W9-CML-887

How Should Prisons Treat Inmates?

Other books in the At Issue series:

MIAMI DADE COLLEGE
Hialeah Campus Library
1780 West 49th Street

WITHDRAWN

(305) 237-8722

How Should Prisons Treat Inmates?

Kristen Bailey, *Book Editor*

Bruce Glassman, *Vice President*
Bonnie Szumski, *Publisher*
Helen Cothran, *Managing Editor*

OPPOSING
VIEWPOINTS®
SERIES

GREENHAVEN PRESS
An imprint of Thomson Gale, a part of The Thomson Corporation

THOMSON
™
GALE

Detroit • New York • San Francisco • San Diego • New Haven, Conn.
Waterville, Maine • London • Munich

© 2005 Thomson Gale, a part of The Thomson Corporation.

Thomson and Star Logo are trademarks and Gale and Greenhaven Press are registered trademarks used herein under license.

For more information, contact
Greenhaven Press
27500 Drake Rd.
Farmington Hills, MI 48331-3535
Or you can visit our Internet site at http://www.gale.com

ALL RIGHTS RESERVED.
No part of this work covered by the copyright hereon may be reproduced or used in any form or by any means—graphic, electronic, or mechanical, including photocopying, recording, taping, Web distribution or information storage retrieval systems—without the written permission of the publisher.

Every effort has been made to trace the owners of copyrighted material.

LIBRARY OF CONGRESS CATALOGING-IN-PUBLICATION DATA

How should prisons treat inmates? / Kristen Bailey, book editor.
   p. cm. — (At issue)
  Includes bibliographical references and index.
  ISBN 0-7377-2719-5 (lib. : alk. paper) — ISBN 0-7377-2720-9 (pbk. : alk. paper)
   1. Prisoners—United States. 2. Imprisonment—United States. I. Bailey, Kristen.
II. At issue (San Diego, Calif.)
HV9471.H68 2005
365'.6'0973—dc22
                                             2004054218

Printed in the United States of America

Contents

Introduction

Incarceration rates have increased steadily in America. The steady growth in the number of prison inmates is due in part to a continued emphasis on tough sentencing for drug-related crimes. The Bureau of Justice Statistics and the National Center on Addiction and Substance Abuse (CASA) estimate that from 60 percent to 83 percent of the nation's inmates have used drugs at some point in their lives, twice the estimated drug use rate of the general population. Additionally, according to a study cited in the *American Journal of Drug and Alcohol Abuse*, by 1998, there were 3.6 times the number of drug offenders being housed in prisons as there were in 1970. This large increase in the number of offenders who are incarcerated due to drug-related crimes, coupled with the high correlation between drug use and other crimes, has filled America's prisons with inmates who are addicted to drugs. Debates about how prisons should treat inmates thus often revolve around the merits and viability of prison drug rehabilitation programs.

Providing rehabilitation services to incarcerated criminals does not come cheap. One county prison system in Pennsylvania decided that providing extensive drug rehabilitation to inmates would double or triple the cost of housing them. Providing that kind of rehab is a "pipe dream," their warden stated, and places "too much of a burden on taxpayers." Many Americans do not want their tax money spent providing drug treatment for the people who have committed crimes. Rather than providing help to prisoners, these citizens feel that it is the job of prisons merely to keep inmates fed, clothed, and locked away. Dr. Jeffrey Schaler, a psychologist and professor at American University, asks why drug treatment in prisons is really necessary: "Prison is a police state so why are there drugs there? If drugs were kept out of prison there would be no need for treatment. Prisoners would be deprived of drugs and that would be the end of it. If (this is) really prison—drugs should not be there." Dr. Schaler further urges Americans to remember what prisons are for before considering spending money to offer drug treatment to inmates: "I believe the purpose of prison should be to protect society from predators we call criminals. We cannot treat them for their criminal behavior because behavior is not a disease."

However, providing treatment to drug-addicted inmates may save taxpayers money in the long run. According to a study of Oregon prisoners cited in *U.S. News & World Report*, every dollar prisons spend on drug rehab saves $5.60 in costs for further prison sentences, welfare, and other expenses. The study reports that the cycle of drug use, arrest, and incarceration can best be broken if prisons pay to provide inmates with quality drug rehabilitation. With treatment for their addictions and education on living drug free, inmates may be better prepared to enter society and become productive, law-abiding citizens, the researchers contend.

But even if Americans could agree that prisoners should be rehabilitated for their addiction to drugs, the fact remains that only a minority of correctional facilities offer drug treatment programs. The Substance Abuse and Mental Health Services Administration's 1997 Survey of Correctional Facilities found that drug and alcohol counseling was available in about 40 percent of federal, state, and local adult and juvenile correctional facilities. That means that 60 percent of inmates do not have drug rehabilitation available in their prisons. Many commentators argue that this dearth of prison drug rehabilitation programs increases recidivism rates and ultimately fosters crime. "We're not protecting the public safety because we aren't treating the problem," said Joseph Califano Jr., former U.S. secretary of health, education and welfare and the president of CASA. "We're supporting the illegal drug market because we are just sending customers back."

The high rates of incarceration for drug-related offenses and the scarcity of prison drug treatment programs have led many Americans to become dissatisfied with the national emphasis on arresting and incarcerating drug abusers. They point out that prisoners arrested for drug-related crimes who do not receive treatment are likely to resume drug use once released and eventually wind up in prison again. Many analysts contend that the war on drugs has not resulted in decreased crime or drug abuse. According to a 1999 study by the American Bar Association, a 73 percent increase in drug arrests between 1992 and 1997 had resulted in no decrease in drug use.

The varied opinions on how prisons should treat inmates often touch upon the issue of prison drug rehabilitation programs. Other issues frequently debated are whether prison labor is inhumane or beneficial to the economy, whether or not inmates should have the right to vote, whether privatization of prisons is beneficial to inmates and taxpayers, and whether super maximum security prisons are humane or needlessly cruel. Debates about how prisoners should be treated are conducted in an effort to make sure that incarceration is handled humanely and results in a safer society.

1

Prisons Are Cruel and Needlessly Punitive

Joseph T. Hallinan

Joseph T. Hallinan has been writing about the criminal justice system for almost a decade. He has won a Pulitzer Prize for journalism and has been named a Nieman Fellow at Harvard University.

In prisons across Alabama, Texas, Georgia, and New York, inmates are tortured, beaten, humiliated, even killed. For all the talk of prisons being like country clubs or resorts, they remain pointlessly violent places. Often, groups of inmates will stand watch, looking for guards, while other large groups of inmates attack or commit crimes against a single prisoner. But the beatings and abuse are not always committed by inmates. Many prisoners are beaten and abused by guards, and occasionally rival groups of inmates will be pitted against one another in fights while guards watch, cheer, and take bets. Rather than rehabilitating inmates, the violent environment in prisons breeds more violence and hatred.

To see how pointlessly punitive the prison experience in America has become, it's worth the trip to Capshaw, Alabama. Capshaw is a tiny town near the Tennessee line, so tiny it has no official population save for the seventeen hundred inmates who occupy the Limestone Correctional Center. Each morning, just after dawn, more than one hundred of them are dragged out of bed and shuffled off to the prison rock pile to begin the state's latest experiment in rehabilitation. Wearing iron shackles around their ankles and safety goggles to protect their

Joseph T. Hallinan, *Going Up the River: Travels in a Prison Nation*. New York: Random House, 2001. Copyright © 2001 by Joseph T. Hallinan. Reproduced by permission of the publisher.

eyes, the men in the chain gang spread out as far as their iron links allow. They grab the yellow-handled sledgehammers, draw them up high, and begin pounding on boulders of limestone, sending stone chips flying through the air. This is their job all day long, five days a week, smashing boulders into rocks.

It is an unnecessary task. The state does not need the rocks, and has had to import more than one hundred tons of boulders just to make the work. The rock will be used, among other things, to pave the road to the cemetery nearby. But in Alabama's prisons, this is what passes for penal innovation. "This is something new in Alabama," says Leoneal Davis, the warden of Limestone. Although it is uncertain how much correction there is in the breaking of a rock, Warden Davis says he is "quite pleased" by what he sees. Rock breaking, he says, "is going to be here to stay."

> **❝** *Hostility breeds violence, and violence breeds fear.* **❞**

In many ways, the Alabama prison system is among the least progressive in the country. Until 1998, the state chained misbehaving inmates to a hitching post, something no other state has done for a quarter century. (It stopped only after a federal judge ruled the practice unconstitutional.) Inmates caught masturbating are made to wear a special uniform, colored flamingo pink. In its renewed emphasis on punishment, however, Alabama is on the cutting edge.

In November 1994, just a few months before Alabama began its rock-breaking experiment, *Reader's Digest* published an article entitled "Must Our Prisons Be Resorts?" The article was written by Robert James Bidinotto, a conservative author from Pennsylvania. . . .

Bidinotto's "Resorts" article told of Massachusetts lifers eating prime rib, of felons in Pennsylvania exercising on aerobic machines, of inmates in New Mexico enjoying conjugal relations with their wives. "Hasn't the time come," Bidinotto asked, "for us to require public officials to explain why prisons need to be resorts?"

Bidinotto's refrain was quickly echoed by politicians around the country, especially those in the South and the West. In 1995,

North Carolina legislators voted to ban TV sets, weight rooms, and outdoor basketball courts. Alabama, Florida, and Arizona reinstituted the chain gang. Other states enacted equally draconian measures. In Mississippi, legislators voted to put inmates back into the striped uniforms of the 1800s. And in South Carolina, the newly elected governor, Republican David Beasley, vowed in his State of the State address to "make prison a place for punishment, a place to which no one would ever want to return."

Many prison professionals cringe when they hear such remarks. They know that many prisons are already intolerable places, that they have been intolerable places for hundreds of years, and that making them more so is only folly. Among their ranks is Frank Wood, the former commissioner of corrections in Minnesota. "Does it seem rational," he says, when I ask him about this trend, "that we should walk down the road, for instance, of creating in our prisons a hell on earth and aggravating the conditions of confinement to the point at which we think we will make prison so miserable that no one will ever want to come back? That's never worked anyplace."

When you take away television, when you take away weights, when you take away all forms of recreation, Wood says, inmates react as normal people would. They become irritable. They become hostile. Hostility breeds violence, and violence breeds fear. And fear, he says, is the enemy of rehabilitation. "You can't create and maintain a climate where people want to change," he tells me, "where every day when they open their cell door at six or seven in the morning they're preoccupied with their survival that day."

> *No attempt is made to monitor the total number of reported sexual assaults inside its [the state of Texas's] prisons, so the frequency is a matter of guesswork.*

Even as Wood spoke, the Florida legislature was debating a bill to require "no-frills" prisons—no TVs, no air-conditioning, no weights. "Our objective," said Representative Randy Ball, one of the bill's supporters, "is to make prison life intolerable."

In pursuit of that objective, inmate treatment programs in

many states have been frozen or gutted. As recently as 1993, for instance, there were nearly 201,000 inmates in drug treatment programs. By 1998, there were only 99,000. Some states, citing low success rates for many treatment programs, abandoned them entirely. In 1994, Governor George Allen of Virginia announced that he would eliminate the $970,000 a year the state spent on sex offender treatment. The move was part of a much broader get-tough program touted by Governor Allen. Under his leadership, Virginia ended parole and ensured that its prison population would expand. In 1995, the Allen administration predicted that the number of prisoners would nearly double in a decade, going from more than 27,000 to 51,300. This expansion led to overcrowded prisons, which led to a demand for more prisons, which led, in the end, to more prison spending. In all, Governor Allen said, the state would need twenty-seven new prisons at a cost of $746 million.

This trend, of course, affected not only Virginia but many other states. In some, prison spending grew so voraciously that it eclipsed spending in other areas, even education. According to a study by the Justice Policy Institute, a liberal research group, and the Correctional Association of New York, between 1988 and 1998 New York State prison spending soared $761.3 million while state allocations for state and city colleges plunged by $615 million—a nearly dollar-for-dollar tradeoff. In California, the researchers reported, prison spending outstripped spending for the state's two premier university systems, the University of California and California State University.

In 1996, researchers at the Rand Corporation, a think tank in Santa Monica, California, published a study comparing the effectiveness of different approaches to crime. They estimated that every $1 million spent incarcerating repeat felons prevented sixty-one serious crimes. By comparison, the same amount spent on high school graduation incentives prevented 258 serious crimes.

Abundant violence

For all the talk of country clubs and resorts, prisons remain violent places. How violent is hard to say because statistics are incomplete. In 1990, the nation's corrections departments reported an average of 239 attacks per year on their guards. By 1997, that figure had risen to 311.

In 1996, sixty-five inmates were reported to have been killed behind bars. But that number probably understates the actual total, according to the Bureau of Justice Statistics, because many states—and the federal government—don't report inmate homicides as a separate offense. Instead, they lump all inmate deaths under one category: "unspecified cause." In 1996, the deaths of 395 inmates were attributed to "unspecified cause."

It is impossible to say how much an atmosphere like this retards rehabilitation.

When it comes to lesser forms of violence, the statistics are even sketchier. There are no reliable reports, for instance, on the number of rapes behind bars, even though, as many prison administrators admit, rape is a common experience. In Texas, no attempt is made to monitor the total number of reported sexual assaults inside its prisons, so the frequency is a matter of guesswork. In 1999, though, several of the state's inmates testified before Judge William Wayne Justice during a trial in U.S. District Court in Houston. Of thirty-two male inmates who testified before the court, at least nine had been sexually assaulted. One inmate testified that after complaining to officers about threats to his safety, he was attacked in the showers by four inmates, three who beat him while one inserted his fingers into the man's rectum. Another inmate testified that he was beaten up by a new cell mate who was "checking him" to see if he would "be a girl." A psychiatrist testified that after another inmate was sexually assaulted, he sought to have his anus sewn shut by a prison doctor.

A vulnerable inmate can easily find himself in a catch-22. To avoid a rape, he must fight. But if he fights—often against more than one opponent—he could suffer a beating far more brutal than the rape itself. But without the evidence of the beating—the bruises, the blood—the guards will not believe a prisoner has been raped, and will not take action.

At the federal trial in Houston, one guard, a captain, was questioned about this paradox:

Q: Now, if an inmate attempts to defend himself [from a sexual assault] and he is fighting an inmate who is maybe stronger and a better fighter than he is, the consequence of that is that he'll get a beating; is that right?

A: Probably so.

Q: And then what's going to happen after the beating?

A: Then that's something that helps me make my decision whether or not his allegations are actually legitimate or not.

Q: Do you think that maybe the inmate just has a choice between a beating and being raped versus just being—you know, he could skip the beating and go right to the rape?

A: That's an individual choice that he can make.

Q: But you disapprove of that choice; is that right?

A: Yes, ma'am, I would.

It is impossible to say how much an atmosphere like this retards rehabilitation. In prison, as Frank Wood suggested, fear trumps everything. A man will do what he must to survive. If he is small and weak, he may decide to become a "punk" and allow himself to be raped by the inmate most likely to protect him. If he has certain skills or connections, he may be invited to join a gang. The gang will protect him, but it will also exact its own price from him—making him a drug "mule," or an enforcer. Or, if he is big enough or brave enough, he may decide to go it alone. This is the riskiest choice and one that will almost certainly require him to fight.

Death behind bars

I got a lesson in this delicate calculus from a brave and determined woman named Vina Payne. Vina lives in Borger, a town of fifteen thousand on the high, empty plains of the Texas panhandle. It is lonesome country, where coyotes trot along fence lines, tumbleweeds blow across the road, and the loudest sound, on most days, is the wind. Vina, one-quarter Choctaw, has shoulder-length black hair and no front teeth. She suffers from high blood pressure, a bad kidney, and a series of lesser ailments. For treatment she drives to the Indian Hospital in Clinton, Oklahoma, a three-hundred-mile round trip. Her husband, Lloyd, was a jet mechanic in Vietnam, and when he got out of the service in 1965 they were married. For the last twenty years Lloyd has been an oil field pumper. All that time, Vina says, he has taken no vacations. Not one. During the boom days of the oil fields, she says, he brought in $8,000 a month. But the boom days are gone. Now Lloyd brings in what he can and Vina works at a convenience store, and they piece together a living.

Sometimes, Vina says, she'll get up at four in the morning and find Lloyd sitting in his favorite chair in their living room, crying in the dark. In 1994, their youngest son, Randy, twenty-three, was killed in prison. His skull was split open by inmates who attacked him with padlocks knotted in socks. Vina has pictures of her son after the attack—hideous color photographs taken at the morgue. She lays them out for me on their kitchen table, fanning them in an arc like a blackjack dealer spreading cards. "I want to have these pictures blowed up," she says, "and have the jury and judge see what they done to my son."

> **In prison . . . fear trumps everything. A man will do what he must to survive.**

Randy was initially assigned to a medium-security prison. But after a few disciplinary infractions, he was shipped out and, on August 4, 1994, landed at the Terrell Unit, [a] Texas prison where Joel Lambright, Jr., had once been a guard. The following day, sometime before 8:30 P.M., three [groups of] inmates cornered him near the showers.

"Basically, what they told him is, 'You're going to pay protection or you're going to fight or you're going to give up sexual favors,'" says Royce Smithey, a prim and pudgy man who works as an investigator for the state's special prison prosecution unit. "And he says, 'Well, I ain't paying you protection and you ain't gonna screw me. So let's get it on, pardner.'

"And that's what he did," Smithey says. "He stayed with 'em for a long time. The guy's pretty tough. He took it as long as he could take it and they finally beat him down and killed him."

Smithey tells me there were at least three groups of inmates involved in the attack. In total, they numbered about twenty. Most of them were armed with padlocks knotted in socks, or with the steel-toed boots issued to inmates on work detail.

"They'd fight for few minutes and quit, then fight for a few minutes and quit," says Smithey. Such attacks are so common, he tells me, inmates have a term for them. "It's called 'holding jiggers.'" That means standing watch while others commit crimes. And that night, while some of the inmates pounded on Randy Payne, others would hold jiggers, making sure no guards came by. And none did. The beating of Randy Payne continued for an hour and a half. During this time not a single guard took notice. The first time a guard noticed anything wrong was when Randy, bloody and incoherent, stumbled into the cellblock's common area.

Randy lingered for a week in the hospital while doctors tried to repair his caved-in skull. Each day, around the clock, Lloyd and Vina stood by his bed. "Last time I seen him," Vina tells me, "his head was held together with metal staples. He had a steel bolt imbedded in his brain. And his face was solid black and blue." On August 12, at 6:15 A.M., Randy died.

The Texas Department of Criminal Justice sent the Paynes a telegram saying it regretted to inform them that their son was dead. The telegram was followed by a small package containing Randy's personal effects: a pair of worn-out tennis shoes, a comb, a toothbrush and toothpaste, a letter from Vina, and a Bible.

For Randy's brother, the box contained only bitterness. At twenty-nine, Roy is the oldest of the surviving Payne children. He is married, with two daughters, and sells cars down at Harner Chevrolet. He has taken his brother's death hard. Sometimes, his mother says, he goes down to the cemetery at midnight and cries at Randy's grave. "In Texas," Roy tells me, "it's no wonder you have so many repeat offenders. It's not a rehabilitation center. It don't rehabilitate 'em. It just gets 'em further in."

His words mirror those of Judge Justice, who presided over the trial in federal court in Houston. At the conclusion of the trial, the judge wrote that the evidence before him "revealed a prison underworld in which rapes, beatings and servitude are the currency of power.

"To expect such a world to rehabilitate wrong-doers," the judge wrote, "is absurd."

> *It is not an overstatement to say that the get-tough mentality breeds more violent prisons.*

Randy's parents do not minimize their son's crimes. He pleaded guilty to burglarizing a building and to indecency with a child, a charge that stemmed from having sex with his girlfriend when he was twenty-one and she was just thirteen. "My son was not perfect," Vina says, "or he would not have been there." Still, she says, "they're crimes he should have paid for, not crimes he should die for." Randy's father nods quietly.

"I'm an honest man," he says later. "I've probably had three or four speeding tickets in my life. I've never been in jail of any kind. I had no idea." Lloyd and I are standing in front of his garage when he tells me this. It is well past dark. Porch lights are on and supper dishes are washed, and Lloyd had intended to walk me to my car. But he lingers along the way, stopping long enough to tell me one more thing about his son.

> *They see a spot of blood, and then here come the sharks everywhere from a mile around.*

"Me and him, when he was little, we used to go cowboyin' together—" but his voice breaks at the thought of them on horseback, and for a long while he is silent. He sniffs once and rubs a knuckle under his nose, then sweeps away a tear with his thick fingers. He draws a big breath through his nose and looks up at the night sky over Texas. People are under the impression that when a man is sent to prison he gets an easy life, Lloyd says. "I think that person should go spend a single day in the prison where my son was."

Guards out of control

It is not an overstatement to say that the get-tough mentality breeds more violent prisons. In 1996, for instance, a bloody mêlée broke out at the Forest Hays, Jr., State Prison in northwestern Georgia. It occurred during an unannounced "sweep" of the prison by a roving squad of riot officers. The officers were led by their commander in chief, a former mortician and state senator named J. Wayne Garner. In 1995, Garner was appointed as the state's commissioner of corrections and soon became one of the nation's most outspoken advocates of getting tough on inmates. Under Garner, no longer were Georgia's penal facilities to be called correctional institutions. With one exception, they were officially renamed state prisons.

Shortly after taking office, Garner made headlines when he said that a third of the inmates in his care "ain't fit to kill." One of his favorite techniques for showing these inmates who was boss involved "sweeps," or shakedown raids, conducted by the department's riot unit. The sweep of Hays was needed, according to Garner's spokesman, because the inmates were not subservient enough. "We had," he said, "to take them down a notch."

According to sworn accounts filed in federal court by guards who were present during the raid, violence erupted after A.G. Thomas, an aide to Garner, grabbed an unresisting inmate by the hair and dragged him across the floor. "When Mr. Thomas did that," said Ray McWhorter, the lieutenant in charge of the tactical squad, "we were all under the impression that it was O.K. to do it. If Mr. Thomas can slam one, then we can slam one, too. That is just the dad-gum way it was."

What followed, Lieutenant McWhorter said, was a bloody free-for-all. Many of the guards had endured years of being spit on, kicked, and otherwise abused by inmates, and when they saw Mr. Thomas grab the inmate, their pent-up rage exploded. "You know how sharks do?" McWhorter said. "They see a spot of blood, and then here come the sharks everywhere from a mile around."

McWhorter's account was supported by the statements of more than half a dozen prison employees at Hays that day, including other guards. Phyllis Tucker, a corrections officer at the prison, said she watched as another guard shoved an inmate's face into a concrete wall. "He screamed," Tucker said. "Blood went up the wall. Blood went all over the ground, all over the inmate. I heard it. It had a sickening, cracking sound."

> *In some instances the wrong inmate—the one complying with the orders to stop fighting—was shot by mistake.*

In all, more than a dozen inmates were beaten that day, some so savagely that even experienced prison workers were upset. After the incident, said Linda Hawkins, a counselor, "I went in my office and I cried."

According to Lieutenant McWhorter's deposition, Garner watched in another cellblock while inmates, some handcuffed and lying on the floor, were punched, kicked, and stomped by guards. Later, according to McWhorter, Garner applauded the officers at a celebratory chicken dinner. "Everybody was high-fiving and shaking hands and congratulating each other and patting each other on the back and bragging about how much butt you kicked."

Garner denied the allegations of abuse, saying later, "I never witnessed it. I was never made aware of it." But in 1998, the state of Georgia agreed to pay $283,000 to settle suits by fourteen inmates who were beaten at Hays. The agreement included "no admission of liability" on the part of Garner or the state. Stephen B. Bright, a lawyer for the inmates and director of the Southern Center for Human Rights in Atlanta, said the incident at Hays was a by-product of the state's get-tough-on-crime politics. "While it may be a great way to play to the crowd," he said, "it's a disastrous way to run a prison."

> *The level of violence . . . was 'totally unacceptable.'*

In New York, much the same approach governs life at the Clinton Correctional Facility, a maximum-security prison known as "Little Siberia" for its isolated setting in Dannemora, near the Canadian border. Clinton holds many of the state's most violent criminals. Most are black or Hispanic and come from tough neighborhoods in New York City. The guards, almost all of them white, are from job-starved Adirondack villages. It is not an easy place to make a living. "You know what your job duties are today?" says Curt Bowman, president of the officers' union. "Go to work. Come out alive."

Between 1990 and 1995, inmates at Clinton won seven federal claims of excessive force by corrections officers, and the state settled ten brutality lawsuits with Clinton inmates rather than defend them in court—a record that corrections experts said was extraordinary. But most of the officers involved in the beatings still work in the prison, in part because disciplinary cases against them, relying as they must on the word of inmates, are hard to prove.

In 1999, California agreed to pay $2.2 million to an inmate who had been shot in the neck and paralyzed by a guard at the California State Prison at Corcoran. The settlement followed disclosures of torture, killings, and cover-ups. Corcoran opened in 1988, a staggeringly large prison built among the cotton fields of the San Joaquin Valley at a cost of $271.9 million. Corcoran was designed to hold twenty-four hundred men, but within a few years of its opening it would hold more than five thousand inmates. As at the Terrell Unit, its officers were green: 70 percent were rookies, fresh out of the academy with only six weeks' training. The men they were asked to guard were some of the worst offenders in California.

Harsh prisons, harsh results

Corcoran swiftly became the deadliest prison in the country. Between 1989 and 1995, forty-three inmates were wounded and seven were killed by officers firing assault weapons—the most killings of inmates in any prison. Rival gang members were pitted against each other in human cockfights watched over by guards. Some of the guards looked forward to the "gladiator days," placing bets while one acted as a ring announcer for the event. But not all guards participated to the same degree. Some guards in the prison's gun posts let the inmates fight until they were exhausted. Others resorted to their rifles almost immediately. In some instances the wrong inmate—the one complying with the orders to stop fighting—was shot by mistake. Each shooting was justified by state-appointed reviewers.

> *To get tough on crime, people had built harsh prisons, and harsh prisons had produced harsh results.*

Inmates were also tortured. Among them was Reginald Cooke, who had spit on an officer and exposed himself to a female guard. In November 1989, guards wanted to inspect his cell. But Cooke wouldn't budge until an "extraction" team of guards came to forcibly remove him. After a brief fight, guards carried Cooke, his arms and legs shackled, to the unit's rotunda. As more than twenty correctional officers watched, a lieutenant ordered Cooke's pants lowered and delivered a jolt to his genitals with an electronic stun gun.

Testifying in court, Daniel McCarthy, the retired director of California corrections, called the violence at Corcoran "absolutely the highest I have ever seen in any institution anywhere in the country." The level of violence, he said, was "totally unacceptable."

There have been similar stories in other states. But after a while they became so similar that they became a blur. Georgia, New York, California, Texas—they were all the same. To get tough on crime, people had built harsh prisons, and harsh prisons had produced harsh results. But no one seemed to care very much. To many people, prisons were still "country clubs." And when stories of violent inmates appeared on the news or in the paper, they were used to justify even more repressive forms of incarceration, no matter how ineffective, no matter how costly.

2

Prisoners Should Not Have It Too Easy

Michael Lockwood and Rachel Alexander

Michael Lockwood is a writer and contributor to the Intellectual Conservative. *Rachel Alexander is the coeditor of IntellectualConservative.com.*

Joe Arpaio, a sheriff in Arizona, has come under fire for the way he runs his prison, leading to general attacks on the harsh treatment of prisoners in America's prisons. Many people talk about prisoners' "rights" but yet cannot explain in legal terms how these rights are being violated in Arpaio's or other prisons. Organizations such as Amnesty International decry the use of restraint chairs, when the truth is only inmates who struggle against these restraints have been hurt. Furthermore, inmates should not have access to free cable, pornography, or a college education when there are many honest citizens who cannot afford such things. Those who argue that prisons should treat inmates better conveniently forget that inmates are criminals who have hurt or killed people.

When asked their opinion of [Arizona] Sheriff Joe Arpaio, most critics dutifully repeat the tired old cliché—he is a publicity hound, and he has violated inmates' rights resulting in their deaths on occasion. Yet when asked to expound, most people cannot explain in legal terms how inmates' rights are being violated.

The truth is that only a very few inmates in Arpaio's jails have been seriously harmed while fighting law enforcement who were trying to restrain them. In fact, these numbers are compa-

Michael Lockwood and Rachel Alexander, "What's Really Happening in Sheriff Joe Arpaio's Jail," *Intellectual Conservative*, March 25, 2002. Copyright © 2002 by *Intellectual Conservative*. Reproduced by permission.

rable to numbers in other county jails around the country. Department of Justice statistics show that there are over 40 accident-related inmate deaths per year in jails across the country. Furthermore, as Maricopa County's Risk Management pointed out, sheriffs are frequently the target of lawsuits, and the number of lawsuits against Arpaio is typical, as indicated by the fact that insurance premiums have not risen.

Unfortunately, there are people with different philosophical beliefs than Arpaio who would rather coddle prisoners by giving them *Hustler* magazines and cable television rather than take the necessary steps to discourage them from returning to their criminal behavior that landed them in jail. Even more shocking is the fact that in many jails and prisons rather than finding methods to discourage criminal behavior, our tax dollars are spent providing criminals with a means to obtain a college degree while in prison. Is it fair that inmates are rewarded for criminal acts while there are honest citizens in our society who cannot even afford to go to college and who are working two jobs to make ends meet?

Exploitation of facts

Because Arpaio's critics have not been able to defeat him in the polls or find any wrongdoing, they resort to blatant distortions of the truth and falsely accuse Arpaio of lying. A favorite tactic used by them is to exploit incidents where inmates who resisted confinement got hurt, portraying them as innocent victims oppressed by the law.

> *Is it fair that inmates are rewarded for criminal acts while there are honest citizens in our society who cannot . . . afford to go to college?*

The most frequently touted example of oppression in Arpaio's jail is the death of Scott Norberg, who died while resisting police officers. Norberg was arrested for chasing after two young girls in Mesa in order to kill them. High on methamphetamine, he attacked the police officers who were trying to restrain him, resulting in his death. Norberg's parents, who had disowned him years ago, filed a lawsuit against the Sheriff's Office. Arpaio defended his officers' actions and wanted to go to trial, but the insurance company insisted on settling. The Justice Department and the FBI conducted an extensive investigation and came up with nothing. Yet this case is typical of those cited constantly by Arpaio's critics as evidence of abuse by the Sheriff's Office.

Arpaio's critics contend that the Sheriff's Office's choice of restraint methods are inhumane. However, as usual, these accusations are baloney. Organizations like Amnesty International decry the use of restraint chairs, since occasionally an inmate who insists on struggling hurts or kills himself in the process. However, even international standards, which are generally more prohibitive than U.S. laws addressing restraint methods, have approved restraint chairs as legitimate uses of restraint when strictly necessary.

> *Torture simply does not include responding to and restraining violent inmates.*

Amnesty International also claims that the Office's use of stun guns is inhumane. However, they conveniently fail to point out that the stun guns were given to the Sheriff's Office by the Department of Justice in a grant program, and both the Department of Justice and the National Sheriff's Association approve of their use. Furthermore, the stun guns are only to be used by law enforcement in self-defense. It is ironic how these so-called compassionate critics say nothing when a guard uses a regular gun in self-defense, killing an attacking inmate, but scream injustice if a guard uses a stun gun in self-defense, briefly stunning the inmate. It's not too difficult to guess which weapon the inmates prefer used.

Arpaio's Office has been accused of cruelty for "hogtying" inmates, a method of restraint that puts the inmates in a painful position. However, hogtying is not allowed in Arpaio's Office. Of course, Arpaio's critics are so eager to accuse Arpaio of oppression that when another local police force in town brought over an inmate it had hogtied, Arpaio's critics took it as yet another opportunity to falsely accuse the Sheriff.

Vague accusations that the Sheriff's Office is "torturing" inmates are embarrassingly incorrect. Even Amnesty International has acknowledged that torture means causing an inmate an extreme level of pain which is repeated in a regular fashion or used for a particular purpose, such as extracting a confession. Torture simply does not include responding to and restraining violent inmates.

> ❝ *Why should the inmates be entitled to free cable, when there are honest citizens who cannot afford cable?* ❞

In response to accusations that his deputies were mistreating inmates, Arpaio installed webcams in the jail so the public could see for themselves. Detractors criticized his webcams as invasions of the right to privacy of pretrial detainees. Yet courts have consistently held that pretrial detainees have a lesser degree of privacy than regular citizens. Pretrial detainees have limited rights, similar to convicted criminals. Funny how these same critics are silent regarding TV police shows that frequently show the faces of people being arrested, and newspaper articles that print the photographs of suspects.

These critics would prefer to have a Pre-Trial Services Agency similar to the one in Pima County [in Arizona], which assesses "risk" levels of arrestees and releases many of them based on this analysis, instead of detaining them overnight. Because Arpaio's Office decides not to immediately release many of the suspects it arrests, the Sheriff's Office is labeled "cruel." But to many members of the public, and to law enforcement, there is a legitimate concern that immediately releasing a man who has violently (but for the first time!) beat up his wife might not be the wisest choice, especially considering he may still be high on drugs. Perhaps it would be safer for the public and his wife to have him sit overnight in jail and cool off.

Rights have not been violated

So far the courts have generally agreed with Arpaio that he has not violated any inmates' rights. The Supreme Court agreed with him that inmates do not have a right to pornography. So maybe Arpaio's critics would be better off protesting the real inhumane treatment of prisoners in other parts of the world. According to Amnesty International's own information, in several countries many pretrial detainees are held for long periods of time before being released. In Venezuela recently, 1,531 unsentenced inmates were held for more than three years in confinement. Inmate deaths are also much worse in other countries. Ten percent of inmates in two Burundi prisons died during the first four months of 1998.

Accusations that Arpaio is a publicity hound are misplaced. Arpaio generates publicity because he implements innovative programs that save taxpayers money and deter criminal behavior. If he was a passive sheriff who simply coddled inmates and gave them their cable television and pornography, so there weren't any complaints, he wouldn't make news. And why should the inmates be entitled to free cable, when there are honest citizens who cannot afford cable? The media's accusations that he seeks out publicity are ironic, considering it is the media who is always calling Arpaio, not the other way around.

Ignoring the good

Arpaio's critics ignore or downplay the good he has done. His drug prevention and treatment program has been a success; a recidivism study found that only eight to ten percent of the 2000 men and women who graduated from it have returned, vastly better than the nation's 60–70% recidivism rate. He started the only high school in the nation for inmates.

Big savings

He has saved taxpayers millions. His volunteer posse of 3,200 is the biggest in the nation and saves taxpayers the cost of paying deputies, costing nothing except for training posse members. Arpaio expanded the posse's duties from typical search and rescue work to rounding up deadbeat parents and rescuing abused animals. He began sheltering abused animals at his jail while their owners awaited trial, and has his female inmates caring for the animals. In 2000, United Animal Nations, a national animal advocacy group, awarded its Animals' Choice Award to Arpaio for his efforts to stop animal cruelty. He has started parenting programs for inmates. His Friday night "smart tents" are available for teachers, parents, and kids to come sleep in overnight to see what being locked up in jail is all about. Children get to see firsthand what it is like to be handcuffed and locked up. The inmates tell them about the dangers of committing crimes.

> *The female inmates also paint curbs, remove graffiti, and pick up litter, saving taxpayers upwards of $500,000 over three years.*

Inmate meals cost 22 cents each, the cheapest in the nation, and are served only twice a day. Most other jails spend $4–5 per day on inmate meals. His detractors claim that Arpaio's figure is exaggerated, and that the actual cost is closer to $1.49 per meal, but they have sneakily reached this figure by including hidden costs like transportation and electricity. His tents cost taxpayers $100,000, a fraction of the $70 million it would have cost to build another jail. His detractors complain that putting inmates in hot tents (which contain swamp coolers) is inhumane, but the inmates say it beats living in one room with 100 other men. When inmates smuggled out 50,000 pairs of underwear, a loss of $40,000 a year, he began providing them with pink underwear to prevent future theft. Sales of the now popular pink underwear have helped pay for costs associated with the posse.

Arpaio's chain gangs are voluntary for the inmates, and save taxpayers money by having the inmates perform work for the county instead of paying regular workers. Contrary to criticism that the chain gang is inhumane, inmates surveyed have said they like working on the chain gang because it gets them outside and gives them something to do. Arpaio's female chain gang is the only female chain gang in the nation. Every Thursday Arpaio lets women volunteer for gravesite duty, which involves digging graves and burying indigents who have died. As the women hear how the indigents died, of drug abuse or other various sad situations, it makes an impact on them. Some of them even pray. The female inmates also paint curbs, remove graffiti, and pick up litter, saving taxpayers upwards of $500,000 over three years.

Critics of Arpaio claim that his tough tactics are not working. Yet the only evidence they can point to that supports this is an Arizona State University study that was improperly conducted. Another tactic frequently used by Arpaio's opponents to discredit him is to find partisan opponents working within his administration, or disgruntled former employees, who have their own agendas and are eager to say whatever it takes to destroy Arpaio's credibility. This is not unusual; within any governmental agency there are going to be naysayers willing to criticize the guy at the top. And for every ex-posse member discovered who complains that the posse is unorganized or costs more than Arpaio says it does, there are twenty posse members who refute the accusations. But hey, for people who have already made up their mind about Arpaio, it's best not to let the facts get in the way of their opinion.

Whatever happened to outrage over crime? It is being replaced with political correctness guised under the important sounding and widely misused mantra of "rights." But the plain fact is, clever word plays don't help the politically correct when their life is being threatened by one of society's degenerates: just like the rest of us, they call the police to defend their rights, not the ACLU [American Civil Liberties Union] to defend their attacker's rights.

3

Taking Away Inmates' Voting Rights Harms Minority Communities

Juan Cartagena, Janai Nelson, and Joan Gibbs

Juan Cartagena is general counsel for the Community Service Society of New York. Janai Nelson is associate counsel at the National Association for the Advancement of Colored People Legal Defense and Educational Fund. Joan Gibbs is general counsel at the Center for Law and Social Justice at Medgar Evers College. The three organizations represent the plaintiffs in Hayden v. Pataki.

New York State's laws, which take away the right to vote from many people convicted of felonies, harms black and Latino communities to a disproportionate degree. In New York convicted felons cannot vote while they are incarcerated or while they are on parole. Because blacks and Latinos are more likely to be sentenced to prison, their voting strength has been unfairly diluted. In addition, the U.S. census counts prisoners as residents of the communities in which they are incarcerated, not as residents of the communities from which they come. These numbers shape decisions that determine state and federal representation. Since all prisons built in the past twenty years are in upstate New York, the voting strength of urban communities of color is further weakened.

O ne of the greatest achievements of the civil rights struggle was the passage of the Voting Rights Act of 1965, which removed most of the obstacles that kept African Americans away

Juan Cartagena, Janai Nelson, and Joan Gibbs, "Felons and the Right to Vote," *The Gotham Gazette*, February 17, 2003. Copyright © 2003 by Juan Cartagena. Reproduced by permission.

from the ballot box and enabled Americans who did not speak English to vote. But the voting rights movement never reached the last excluded segment of our democracy: our prisoners.

A legal action filed [in early 2003] seeks to fill that gap in voting rights law. It argues that New York State's laws that take the right to vote away from many people convicted of felonies disproportionately harms black and Latino communities. As a result, these laws violate the Constitution, the Voting Rights Act and international law.

> *The disproportionate arrest, conviction, and imprisonment of African Americans and Latinos has diluted minority voting strength in New York State.*

Currently, 1.4 million African American men in the country—13 percent of all black men—are disenfranchised because of a felony conviction. This is seven times the rate for all Americans.

While laws vary from state to state, in New York only convicted felons who serve time in prison lose their right to participate in the democratic process. They cannot vote for the entire time they remain behind bars and for any time they are out of jail on parole, when they are required to check in regularly with an officer and meet various other requirements. People convicted of felonies but sentenced to alternatives to prison such as probation retain their right to vote.

Disproportionate numbers

In New York, race and ethnicity have a lot to do with whether a convicted felon gets sent to prison. Blacks found guilty of felonies are twice as likely as their white counterparts to be sentenced to prison as opposed to probation. Blacks comprise less than 16 percent of New York State's population but account for almost 51 percent of the 71,000 people in prison and 50 percent of those on parole. Latinos, about 15 percent of the state population, are almost 30 percent of the prison population and 32 percent of those on parole.

The disproportionate arrest, conviction, and imprisonment

of African Americans and Latinos has diluted minority voting strength in New York State since only incarceration triggers the denial of voting rights.

Our three organizations seek to change this. The NAACP Legal Defense and Educational Fund, the Community Service Society of New York and the Center for Law and Social Justice at Medgar Evers College have filed a class action lawsuit charging that New York State laws denying the vote to individuals who are incarcerated or on parole are unconstitutional and discriminatory. They argue that these laws were originally intended to deny full rights to African Americans, and their continued application today disproportionately harms black and Latino communities.

The suit, *Hayden v. Pataki,*[1] was initially filed in September, 2001, by Joseph Hayden while he was a prisoner in New York. Hayden, who is now on parole, was to represent all black and Latino prisoners denied the right to vote.

> **❝** New York State has a long history of racial discrimination in its voting laws. **❞**

Now the three organizations want to add three groups to the original complaint: blacks and Latinos incarcerated on a felony conviction, blacks and Latinos on parole for a felony conviction, and black and Latino voters from specific communities in New York City who are collectively denied an equal opportunity in the political process because of the disproportionate disenfranchisement of African Americans and Latinos. These communities include East Harlem, Washington Heights, the Lower East Side, Hunts Point, Morrisania, Soundview, Central Brooklyn, East New York, Jamaica and St. Albans.

The request to expand the Hayden case was made to the U.S. District Court for the Southern District of New York [in early 2003]. The court is awaiting a response from the governor's office and the New York State Board of Elections, the defendants in the case. Then it will decide whether to allow the expansion.

New York State has a long history of racial discrimination in its voting laws. Like so many other states, New York enacted

1. This case was ongoing as this volume went to press.

these laws when racial discrimination against African Americans was legal and commonplace. As far back as 1777, the framers of the state's first constitution gave only free men and property holders the right to vote.

> *Some argue that people who violate the law should not have a say in determining what the laws should be.*

In 1821, as a limited number of blacks became free men and property holders, the state constitution was changed to explicitly apply higher property requirements only to men of color. That same year, the state constitution was amended to deny the vote to anyone convicted of what it called "any infamous crime." By the mid-1800's, the "infamous crime" disqualification was renewed in New York State with the full understanding that blacks were 13 times more likely than whites to commit an "infamous crime."

It took the Civil War and the passage of the 15th Amendment to the U.S. Constitution to nullify these laws. Nevertheless, New York State re-enacted the "infamous crime" provision in 1894. This antiquated provision still remains in our State Constitution and is interpreted today to include all felonies, i.e., crimes that may result in jail sentences of one year or more.

Official discrimination against African American and Latino citizens in New York continued throughout the 20th century with literacy tests, English-only election procedures and discriminatory purging of voter rolls. It took the Voting Rights Act to restore a fair election structure in New York. The act targeted three counties in New York City—Bronx, Kings, and New York—requiring special measures to guard against discriminatory voting laws and policies. These provisions remain in force today.

Disproportionate disenfranchisement is made even worse by the fact that the U.S. Census counts prisoners as residents of the communities in which they are incarcerated, not as residents of the communities from which they come. The state uses these Census numbers to shape redistricting decisions that determine state and federal representation. Since all prisons built in New York State since 1982 are upstate, the voting strength of communities of color—mostly located in New York City—is further weakened.

Some argue that people who violate the law should not have a say in determining what the laws should be. Others fear that including convicted felons in the body politic would weaken law enforcement institutions. Senator Mitch McConnell of Kentucky has remarked that allowing convicted felons to vote would mean that "rapists, murderers, robbers and even terrorists or spies" could vote.

Prisoners want a voice

These arguments reflect the typical knee-jerk reaction against anything that appears, however minimally, to benefit persons convicted of crimes. In fact, allowing persons who are convicted of crimes to vote may make it less likely a person will break the law again. After all, voting gives people a stake in society and reflects the basic truth about what it means to be a citizen of the United States.

Prisoners and parolees are merely seeking a voice in society. They ask rightfully: What is America afraid of? What legitimate penal interest is served by taking away our vote, our badge of citizenship?

The United States incarcerates more people per capita than any other country in the world. Eighteen European democracies permit incarcerated prisoners to vote, as do Canada and Puerto Rico. In the U.S., only the states of Maine and Vermont do so. No democracy other than the United States bars parolees from voting.

Martin Luther King once wrote, "No nation can long continue to flourish or to find its way to a better society while it allows any one of its citizens to be denied the right to participate in the most fundamental of all privileges of democracy—the right to vote." At the time—1965—King was referring to the need for a law that would ensure the right of all African Americans to vote. But his words apply today to the effects of New York State's discriminatory disenfranchisement laws.

4

Supporters of Inmates' Right to Vote Have Ulterior Motives

Peter Kirsanow

Peter Kirsanow is a member of the U.S. Commission on Civil Rights.

Around 4 million felons and inmates in the United States have temporarily or permanently lost their voting rights. The case for felons being allowed to vote is championed by a growing number of politicians and special interest groups. These proponents are motivated not by altruism but by politics; felons vote overwhelmingly for Democrats, thus liberal politicians and organizations have a vested interest in granting them voting rights. Moreover, these voting rights advocates gain sympathy for their cause by charging that voting rules unfairly disenfranchise blacks, who are disproportionately represented in the criminal justice system. However, these advocates are not concerned with minorities' rights—they merely want liberals to win the next election.

Wesley Clark recently told a black audience in Birmingham, Alabama that states should restore the right to vote to felons who've completed their sentences. Clark's not alone. Several Democrats . . . support felon voting.

A cynic may be forgiven for suspecting that the motivation behind such support has as much to do with political expediency as principle. . . . While it's unlikely that [future] election[s] will be as close as that of 2000, minor shifts in demographics and

Peter Kirsanow, "The Felon Franchise," *National Review Online*, January 8, 2004. Copyright © 2004 by United Feature Syndicate, Inc. Reproduced by permission.

voting patterns could have a dramatic, if not decisive, effect. This is particularly true in the case of felon voting, a cause championed by a growing number of politicians and interest groups.

The estimates of the number of people who have either temporarily or permanently lost the right to vote due to felony convictions vary, but most agree that the figure hovers around four million. Forty-eight states currently have some form of restriction on the right of felons to vote. The exceptions are Maine and Vermont, which even permit inmates to vote. Thirty-three states disenfranchise felons who are on parole. Eight states deny felons the right to vote for life.

What might have been

Several recent studies contend that even allowing for their expected lower participation rates, the restoration of voting rights to felons would have shifted the outcome of a number of recent congressional elections. This tantalizes the felon-vote movement. But the movement receives its greatest inspiration from the 2000 election fiasco in Florida. Felon-vote proponents claim that had felons who have completed their sentences been permitted to vote in Florida, [Al] Gore would be president today. And they're probably right.

As David Lampo has noted, a study by sociologists Christopher Uggen of the University of Minnesota and Jeff Manza of Northwestern [University] shows that felons vote overwhelmingly for Democrats—at a rate approaching 70 percent. (In fact, this estimate may be low. In some Florida counties more than 80 percent of the felons who voted illegally were registered Democrats.) Therefore, had Florida's felons voted in the 2000 presidential election at a rate comparable to the rest of the Florida electorate, [Democrat] Al Gore would have won the state by more than 60,000 votes. . . .

Restoration of rights

[In 2004] the state's department of corrections settled a lawsuit by felon-advocacy groups to ease restoration of voting rights for felons who've completed their sentences. (Florida bars felons from voting unless their rights have been restored by executive clemency.) Pursuant to the settlement, the state will provide advice and assistance to felons regarding the restoration process. According to the *Naples Daily News*, Florida officials estimate that nearly 130,000 felons should have their voting rights restored in the near future.

> *A cynic may be forgiven for suspecting that the motivation behind . . . support [for voting rights] has as much to do with political expediency as principle.*

The restoration of voting rights to felons is decidedly unpopular with the electorate. For example, in 1998, more than *80 percent* of Utah voters approved a measure to bar inmates from voting. In 2000, the Massachusetts electorate, among the most liberal in the country, voted for a constitutional amendment barring felon inmates from voting.

An issue of race?

But overwhelming public opposition has not deterred felon-vote advocates. They've simply resorted to a receptive judiciary to achieve their objective. Several recent lawsuits throughout the country assert that state felon-disenfranchisement laws violate Section 5 of the Voting Rights Act and the equal-protection guarantees in state constitutions. Typical among these suits is *Farrakhan v. State of Washington*, a case that had been dismissed by the U.S. District Court in Spokane, but revived a short time ago by the Ninth Circuit. *Farrakhan* was brought by minority inmates challenging the state of Washington's constitutional prohibition against voting by imprisoned felons. The inmates maintain that racial disparities in the state's criminal-justice system effectively result in a denial of the right to vote on the basis of race. The court noted that while constituting only 3 percent of the state's population, blacks represent 37 percent of those adjudicated "persistent offenders." The Ninth Circuit remanded the case to the district court for a full hearing on the issue of whether racial bias in the criminal-justice system, combined with the denial of voting rights to inmates, violates the Voting Rights Act.

The racial-disparity argument is a recurrent theme in challenges to felons' voting prohibitions. Claims of racial discrimination tend to generate greater public concern than complaints that murderers and rapists won't get to elect the next president. Felon-vote advocates recite the statistic that nearly 1.5 million black men are prohibited from voting due to felony convictions. The Sentencing Project maintains that black men are disenfranchised by state restrictions on felon voting at a rate seven times the national average. The group asserts that at current incarceration rates, in some states as many as 40 percent of black men will soon be disenfranchised. These figures are clearly disconcerting, but for reasons more fundamental than the inability of felons to vote.

As might be expected, the issue has captured the attention of some in Congress. Representative John Conyers (D., Mich.) introduced the Civil Participation and Rehabilitation Act of 1999. The bill had 37 cosponsors and sought to provide federal voting rights to all felons released from prison, regardless of whether their respective states barred them from voting. The bill was referred to the Subcommittee on the Constitution, and went nowhere.

> *Forty-eight states currently have some form of restriction on the right of felons to vote.*

Conyers reintroduced the bill in January 2003. The list of cosponsors dropped to 25, but still boasted many members of the Congressional Black Caucus along with Democratic presidential aspirant Dennis Kucinich.

The bill's findings prominently cite some of the racial disparities noted above. The purpose of the findings is to provide Fourteenth Amendment support for overriding state restrictions on felon voting. But franchise qualifications are generally the prerogative of the states. It's unlikely that a racially neutral felon-disenfranchisement law (without discriminatory intent) that has a racially disparate impact would violate the equal-protection clause. (Such a law's validity under the Voting Rights Act is another inquiry altogether.)

Distinctions among the disenfranchised

Most state disenfranchisement laws don't have blanket prohibitions against felon voting. Distinctions are made between inmates and releasees, parolees and probationers, etc. Some states even differentiate between first offenders and repeat offenders. Most people grasp the reasoning underlying these distinctions: Denying the franchise to a violent repeat offender is a bit different than denying it to a youthful, one-time drug offender. And many find distasteful the prospect of politicians pandering to the interests of criminals. (What might a governor facing recall promise tens of thousands of inmates in exchange for their votes? Pardons? Weekend furloughs?)

States may plausibly deny the franchise to murderers on the basis that they have permanently disenfranchised their victims, or to violent criminals because they generally have high recidivism rates. These rationales may not be exemplars of logical perfection, but they are no less defensible than those for denying felons a number of other rights (certain categories of employment, child custody, firearms ownership, etc.)

On the other hand, a state may decide that certain classes of felons should regain the right to vote because it assists their reintegration into society. Denying an 18-year-old the right to vote for the rest of his life because of a nonviolent crime is unlikely to act as either a deterrent or enhance the integrity of the political process.

As David Lampo notes, these distinctions are immaterial to many felon-vote advocates. Their aim is nothing less than the wholesale restoration of voting rights to all convicts—and that suggests an agenda that's more partisan than altruistic.

5

Private Prisons Benefit Inmates

Matthew Mitchell

Matthew Mitchell is a research economist for the New Mexico–based Rio Grande Foundation. He is currently working on a doctorate in economics at George Mason University.

Two-thirds of all states now house some of their prisoners privately. Those states have found that private prisons are just as safe, if not safer than their public counterparts. It has also been found that conditions in private prisons are just as or more humane than those of public prisons. Evidence has shown that this high quality of incarceration can be delivered at a lower cost. Private prison managers have much more personal motivation to push for gains in quality and efficiency.

The notion of privately operated prisons may seem radical given the United States' long history of publicly operated correctional facilities. But in recent years, several states have experimented with privately run correctional facilities. Those states have found that private prisons are responsive to policymakers' demands for secure, humane facilities; they house inmates with less expense than a traditional public prison system; and they encourage cost savings in their publicly operated counterparts. Given Maryland's ongoing budget crisis and growing concerns about the safety and conditions of its prison system, now may be a good time for the Old Line State to consider this idea.

The cost savings from privatizing a portion of Maryland's prison system would be significant. If the state were to implement a modest program of housing just five percent of its in-

Matthew Mitchell, "Can Maryland Benefit from Privatizing Some of Its Prison System?" *Maryland Policy Report*, March 24, 2004. Copyright © 2004 by the Maryland Public Policy Institute. Reproduced by permission.

mates in privately run prisons, experience from elsewhere suggests Maryland could save $97 million per year. A broader effort that would place 45 percent of inmates in private institutions could save $230 million annually. That is a significant savings that could be redirected toward public safety or other state operations.

Moral concerns

Before Maryland can consider the financial benefits of using privately run prisons, it should first consider whether such facilities are morally acceptable. At first blush, the idea that one person may profit from another's incarceration may seem inhumane. But in a free society of voluntary exchange, it is impossible to separate profit from any sort of good or service—including the operation of a prison. In state institutions, guards are paid to watch the prisoners, administrators are paid to run the facilities, and other employees provide services from preparing the food to washing the sheets. Each of those employees is motivated to do that work by the compensation he or she receives—that is, by the opportunity to profit personally. If it is morally acceptable for each of a prison's many employees to be motivated by profit, then it seems strange to claim that the employees cannot bind together as a corporation backed by investors and pursue profit for their combined work.

> *Those states have found that private prisons are responsive to policymakers' demands for secure, humane facilities.*

If the managers of a public correctional facility and a private correctional facility both seek profit, what distinguishes the two? In a word: competition. Relatively insulated from public demands and economic incentive, public prison managers have less personal motivation than their private counterparts to push for gains in quality and efficiency. On the other hand, private prison officials know that if they fail to offer a quality product at a reasonable price, their contract will not be renewed but will instead go to another bidder. Given the incentive structure that private prison managers face, one would expect them to offer higher quality services at lower cost than their publicly operated counterparts.

Experiences elsewhere

In 1993, Baltimore's state jails were placed under a court order to improve sanitation and medical care within the system. A decade later, two watchdog groups filed court papers contending that the state had failed to live up to that obligation. Maryland's department of corrections is hardly the first to be found in violation of the Constitution's prohibition against cruel and unusual punishment. Reason Public Policy Institute researchers Geoffrey Segal and Adrian Moore, in their 2002 paper "Weighing the Watchmen," noted, "In 2001, of the 50 state correctional departments, 13 entire departments were under a court order to relieve unsatisfactory conditions." On the other hand, not a single private prison had been placed under a court order for unsatisfactory conditions as of 2001.

> **❝** *In a free society of voluntary exchange, it is impossible to separate profit from any sort of good or service.* **❞**

Another way to measure quality is through accreditation rates. The American Correctional Association is an independent, non-profit, professional corrections organization that accredits public and private prisons on such dimensions as staff training, adequacy of medical services, sanitation, use of segregation, incidents of violence, crowding, offender activity levels, programs, and provisions of basic services that may impact the life, safety, and health of inmates and staff. As of 2001, 44 percent of all private prisons were accredited. Just 10 percent of public prisons were accredited.

There is also evidence from a number of independent studies that indicate that private prisons offer higher quality services. According to Segal and Moore, 16 of the 18 studies they reviewed found that private prisons perform as well as or better than public prisons when judged on quality.

The evidence suggesting private prisons save money is also robust. Many of the state laws that initially authorized private prisons also required cost-analysis studies. Consequently, there is a large body of scholarship that has found private prisons to be less expensive than their public counterparts. Segal and Moore identified 28 private prison cost studies and noted that "virtually all of them found private prisons to provide significantly lower cost—on average between five and 15 percent."

Statistical analysis

A statistical analysis I recently conducted provides further evidence in support of those findings. . . . I compared the entire budgets of 46 state departments of corrections. (I could not use all 50 states because some of the relevant data were unavailable.) Specifically, I was searching to see if, in states where private prisons operated, public prisons responded by finding ways to cut their costs. If they did, then taxpayers realized a "double savings" from private prisons—the lower cost of the private prisons themselves and the reduced cost of the public prisons that responded to the competition.

> *Private prison officials know that if they fail to offer a quality product at a reasonable price, their contract will not be renewed.*

To measure the extent of privatization, the study relied on the percentage of prisoners in privately managed prisons in each state. I had to control for a number of factors that would have distorted the findings and produced misleading results. (Of particular concern are factors outside the control of prison managers.) One of those factors is the state-to-state difference in the market wage for prison personnel. I accounted for that factor by relying on the entry-level pay of state police officers; because state police officers are drawn from roughly the same labor market as prison guards, it is reasonable to expect state police pay to mirror prison guard pay. I also adjusted for discrepancies in labor conditions caused by the existence of right-to-work legislation. One would expect the freer labor market of a right-to-work state to translate into lower per-prisoner cost, and I did not want that to distort my findings. Finally, by factoring in prison crowding, I controlled for state-to-state differences in a prison's ability to use its capacity. If a warden can place more prisoners in a given space, he can save money on important variable costs such as guards, surveillance equipment, and even electricity. But prison managers face different state laws and court rulings that govern the legally permissible crowding level. Furthermore, states differ in their fiscal outlook and ability to match growth in prison populations with new prisons. Other factors being equal, one would expect that in a state where relatively high prison densities are possible, the prison managers can lower per-prisoner cost by increasing density, but again, I did not want that to distort my findings. . . .

> *They have also found that the conditions in private prisons are just as humane and in many cases more so than in public prisons.*

Other factors held constant, states with five percent of their prisoners under private management spent about $4,084 less per prisoner in 2001 than non-privatized states. That is fully 14 percent of median per-prisoner spending in 2001. What is more, as the percentage of privatization increased, states tended to spend even less per prisoner. A 45 percent privatized state, for example, spent $9,660 less per prisoner in 2001 than a non-privatized state. That is nearly a third of what the median-spending state spent per prisoner in 2001.

Private prisons in Maryland

Given the results above, we can predict how much savings Maryland would realize at various levels of privatization. The Old Line State's prison population is roughly 24,000, which would allow considerable savings. If Maryland were to follow the general trend, then five percent privatization in 2001 would have saved $97 million dollars, or 11 percent of that year's Department of Corrections budget. Forty-five percent privatization would have saved $230 million, fully 27 percent of the 2001 corrections budget. . . .

Savings of that size would be quite helpful, especially given Maryland's current budget situation. The Old Line State suffered through a $550 million shortfall in 2003 followed by a

$1.2 billion deficit in 2004. If 45 percent of Maryland's prisoners were housed privately, the state's 2003 deficit would have been 40 percent smaller. Moreover, when the state does return to fiscal health, the use of privately operated prisons would allow Maryland to reallocate corrections money to other uses like law enforcement, education, and public health.

However, at the moment, there is little political impetus in the Old Line State to use private prisons. This is understandable; the idea is a departure from the nation's centuries-old tradition of publicly operated prisons. But policies have evolved in recent years. Two-thirds of all states now house some of their prisoners privately. Those states have found that private prisons are just as safe, if not more so, than their public counterparts. They have also found that the conditions in private prisons are just as humane and in many cases more so than in public prisons. Finally, there is considerable evidence that private prisons deliver this better product at a lower cost. If Maryland pursued this innovative idea, it could expect similar results. But, until the state does, prisoners and taxpayers will continue to pay the price of the status quo.

6

Private Prisons Harm Inmates

Jenni Gainsborough

Jenni Gainsborough is the director of the Washington office of Penal Reform International.

Corrections Corporation of America (CCA), the nation's largest operator of for-profit prisons, has just celebrated its twentieth anniversary. Unfortunately, CCA prisons are horribly mismanaged. They fail to control inmate violence, offer prisoners inadequate health care, and are subject to prisoner escapes. Moreover, they treat prison employees poorly. The only way a private prison can sell itself to government as a cheaper option than public prisons is to use as little staff as possible, pay them minimum salaries, and spend very little on training.

Corrections Corporation of America (CCA), the nation's largest operator of prisons for profit, is celebrating its 20th anniversary throughout [2003] "at both the company's corporate Nashville office and at all of the more than 60 prisons, jails and detention centers under CCA ownership and/or management."

No word on whether the prisoners will be celebrating with them. However, a new report from Grassroots Leadership [a small, nonprofit organization dedicated to abolishing for-profit private prisons] sticks a pin in their birthday balloon with a very critical look at the company's management of both its financial affairs and its contract prisons.

It is no secret that CCA has had its financial problems over the years. It came close to insolvency in the late 1990s after it

Jenni Gainsborough, "The Truth About Private Prisons," www.AlterNet.org, December 15, 2003. Copyright © 2003 by the Independent Media Institute. All rights reserved. Reproduced by permission.

accumulated heavy debt building expensive speculative prisons and restructuring itself as a real estate investment trust. After restructuring again, shaking up its upper management and spending $120 million to settle investor lawsuits, the company now claims to be in better financial shape. The report concedes that there has been some improvement but remains unconvinced about the company's long-term viability especially as many states are trying to reduce the size of their prison populations.

> *The company's failures as a prison operator . . . are the most worrying.*

For those who are more concerned about the public policy implications of the CCA story than the ups and downs of its investors, the company's failures as a prison operator and its successes in influencing penal policy at the state and federal level are the most worrying areas of the report.

Is private really better?

For-profit prison companies like CCA have always presented themselves as both cheaper and better than the traditional publicly owned prisons, staffed by state employees. However, from the mayhem and murders at the prison in Youngstown, Ohio, which eventually led to the company paying $1.6 million to prisoners to settle a lawsuit, to a series of wrongful death civil suits, and numerous disturbances and escapes, the authors document in detail a staggering range of failures of prison management.

- failure to provide adequate medical care to prisoners;
- failure to control violence in its prisons;
- substandard conditions that have resulted in prisoner protests and uprisings;
- criminal activity on the part of some CCA employees, including the sale of illegal drugs to prisoners; and
- escapes, which in the case of at least two facilities include inadvertent releases of prisoners who were supposed to remain in custody.

Many of the company's problems are blamed on its labor policies. Because prisons are very labor intensive institutions, the only way a company like CCA can sell itself to government as a cheaper option than public prisons while still making a profit, is by using as few staff as possible, paying them as little as possible, and not spending much on training.

From the beginning, CCA has sought to depress its labor costs by keeping wages low and by denying its employees traditional (defined-benefit) pension plans. One predictable result of these policies has been understaffing and high rates of turnover at some of its facilities. For example, annual turnover rates at several CCA facilities in Tennessee have been more than 60 percent. Another, equally predictable, has been the opposition of public service unions to the spread of prison privatization. Criminal justice reformers, trying to reduce the use of incarceration in the U.S., don't normally find themselves allying with prison guard unions but in this fight they are all on the same side.

Money talks

Despite this opposition, CCA has been quite successful in recent years in influencing the public debate and winning the support of legislators. Of course, it is not hard to win legislators when you back up your arguments with hard cash. The company spends hundreds of thousands of dollars during each state election cycle to try to gain access and build support for its projects. At the federal level, CCA has given more than $100,000 in soft money to the Republican Party since 1997 as well as political action committee contributions to individual members of key Congressional committees.

> // *The authors [of the report on private prisons] document in detail a staggering range of failures of prison management.* //

The presence of J. Michael Quinlan, the former head of the Federal Bureau of Prisons, among CCA's senior executives has surely helped the growth in its contracts with the Federal Bureau of Prisons, and the expectation of further expansion as more prisons for immigrants are planned. In its home state of Tennessee, CCA has enjoyed close relationships with many powerful public figures, including governors. And the for-profit prison companies have their own trade association lobbying for them on Capitol Hill—the Association of Private Correctional and Treatment Organizations (APCTO).

While all of that might be dismissed as no more than the typical business-building efforts of any company looking to make a profit for its shareholders, there are other more troubling aspects to CCA's behavior.

Questionable research

One has been its use of research from dubious sources to push its claims of superiority and cost-savings for the private sector. Much of it is produced by researchers who are either funded by the industry or are ideologically predisposed in favor of privatization. For example, Charles Thomas, director of the supposedly neutral Private Prison Project of the University of Florida who was widely quoted as an expert on prison privatization throughout the 90s, served on the board of CCA and received several millions of dollars in consulting fees from them.

> *The U.S. certainly does not need companies with a vested financial interest in [prison] growth influencing our justice policies.*

More recently, a study published in the Harvard Law Review was touted as an independent academic study of privatization. None of its boosters, however, mentioned that the author, in addition to being a graduate student at Harvard, is associated with the Reason Public Policy Institute, a division of the Reason Foundation whose purpose is to promote the privatization of public services.

Perhaps most controversial is CCA's close ties to the American Legislative Exchange Council (ALEC). ALEC is a powerful force in the promotion of the conservative policy agenda among state legislators. One of its major functions is writing model bills that advance conservative principles and working with its members to have these bills introduced. CCA has been a corporate member and a major contributor to ALEC and a member of its Criminal Justice Task Force. CCA executives have co-chaired the Task Force over many years. As a result of the model bills developed by the Task Force, ALEC claims credit for the widespread adoption of Truth in Sentencing and Three Strikes/Habitual Offender legislation. Through its support of ALEC, CCA is helping to create greater demand for its services as a result of changes in state policies that keep more people behind bars for longer periods.

Although this aspect of its work is not given a major emphasis in the report, it surely represents the most troubling impact of for-profit prison companies. With more than two million people behind bars and the highest rate of incarceration in the world, the U.S. certainly does not need companies with a vested financial interest in further growth influencing our justice policies.

Growth despite problems

As Grassroots Leadership's report so fully documents, CCA has little to be proud of in its 20-year-history. Unfortunately, the problems that have dogged it are unlikely to stand in the way of its growth, particularly at the federal level where its pro-privatization, pro-incarceration policies are mirrored by the current [George W. Bush] administration. Even at the state level, where the report optimistically suggests that declining prison populations will hurt the company, there are signs that cash-strapped state governments are again turning to the private sector to solve short-term problems without any consideration to the long-term impacts.

And even though CCA itself has pulled back from the international arena after a number of well publicized problems, the model of prison privatization it developed is still being sold to nations in transition that can ill afford either the social or economic costs associated with profit-driven prison growth.

CCA may believe it has much to celebrate. The rest of us have good reason to hold our applause.

7

Prison Labor Benefits Inmates and the Economy

Robert D. Atkinson

Robert D. Atkinson is vice president of the Progressive Policy Institute and director of its Technology and the New Economy project.

Prison labor is good for prisoners and the U.S. economy. Prisoners who work have lower rates of recidivism, and they appreciate the chance to spend their time doing something more interesting and lucrative than watching television. Prison labor increases total employment and gross domestic product and will not reduce private sector employment levels. The revenues from prison work can also pay for the cost of housing inmates.

[In 2002,] six years after President [Bill] Clinton signed legislation ending welfare as we know it, which replaced the unconditional entitlement to cash aid with temporary cash aid conditioned on work, it is ironic that there is one major group in society that still gets public support without a work requirement—prisoners. While our nation has made great strides in the last few years to move welfare recipients from dependency to work, surprisingly, we're moving in the other direction when it comes to transitioning prisoners to paid work. Fearing competition from prison labor, union and business interests have mounted an aggressive lobbying campaign to roll back paid prison labor, in spite of the fact that it can provide convicts with

Robert D. Atkinson, "Prison Labor: It's More than Breaking Rocks," *Policy Report*, May 2002. Copyright © 2002 by the Progressive Policy Institute. Reproduced by permission.

useful skills they can use upon release while at the same time helping to offset some of the cost of housing prisoners.

While the number of prison workers has increased over the years, only a modest share of state and federal inmates work at jobs for pay. There are approximately two million prison and jail inmates in the United States. The Federal Prison Industries (an arm of the Federal Bureau of Prisons) employs approximately 23,000 inmates out of a total of 157,000 prisoners. Approximately 65,000 inmates work in state prisons, but only 3,700 prisoners (in 36 states) are employed by private-sector companies.

Prison labor is good for the economy

Even though the number of prison inmate workers is relatively small (less than one-fiftieth of 1 percent of the civilian workforce), opposition to prison labor has been growing from affected industries and unions. Both groups not only actively oppose expansion of prison labor, but have supported legislation to dramatically restrict the programs run by Federal Prison Industries (FPI). Both argue that the current situation provides unfair competition. This view has gained increased credibility among policymakers, in part based on the inaccurate view that prison labor versus civilian labor is a zero-sum game and that growth in one comes at the expense of the other. Applying a growth economics framework, it is clear that expansion of prison labor can be good for the U.S. economy, increasing total employment and Gross Domestic Product (GDP), while not reducing private sector employment levels.

> *"Just as Congress should not give in to protectionists on trade, they should not give in to protectionists on prison labor."*

Just as Congress should not give in to protectionists on trade, they should not give in to protectionists on prison labor. There are three main reasons why Congress should expand, not reduce, prison labor. First, there is clear evidence that prisoner work requirements lead to lower recidivism. Second, the revenue from prison work can and should pay for the costs of housing them in prisons as well as victim restitution, child support, and the like. Finally, because it leads to increased production of goods and services, prison labor helps spur the U.S. economy. Notwithstanding the fact that prison labor can be good for both prisoners and the economy, the current FPI program is in need of significant reform. A new prison policy should:

- allow private sector companies to employ prisoners in state and federal prisons at least at the minimum wage to make virtually whatever product or service they want to and sell it to whomever they choose;
- lift federal restrictions on the interstate transportation of goods and services produced in state prisons;
- subject federal and state prison workplaces to Occupational Safety and Health Administration (OSHA) inspections;
- institute an FPI ombudsman program to investigate complaints by workers about unfair working conditions;
- extend the Trade Adjustment Assistance Act to cover workers displaced by prison labor; and
- mandate that all federal prisoners who can work do work, provided that work is available.

The history of prison labor

Prison labor has its roots in the 1800s, when inmates worked for private companies without pay. For example, by 1890, convict leasing in Alabama had become a significant operation, particularly focused on black prisoners. (White men usually remained inside the penitentiary or local jail.) In other cases, such as a labor dispute at the Tennessee Coal Company in 1891, prison labor was used to break strikes. Prison labor was not about rehabilitation or fostering a safer prison environment, it was about getting revenue to pay for prisons. And not surprisingly, given the lack of legal and other safeguards at the time, there were significant abuses. After hundreds of prisoners in various states died on the job due to hazardous conditions, unions and prison reformers rightly demanded a halt to the practice.

As in so many policy areas, the federal government got involved in the issue during the New Deal era. The 1935 Hawes-Cooper Act created FPI as an arm of the Federal Bureau of Prisons and allowed it to employ federal prisoners in making goods for sale to the federal government. However, because the legislation was passed during the Depression and was motivated by the fear that private jobs would be lost to prison labor, it outlawed interstate trade in convict-made goods (except if sold to the federal government) and placed a number of other restrictions on FPI.

In response to the need to provide prisoners with more work opportunities, Congress passed the Justice System Improvement Act in 1979. Among other things, the Act repealed a number of the limitations imposed by the Hawes-Cooper Act and created the Prison Industry Enhancement Certification Program that allows prisons to link up with private companies. In particular, the bill permitted states to create prison work programs whereby prisoners would be eligible to be employed by private companies. Deductions could be made for room and board, federal and state taxes, family support, contributions to a state's crime victim fund, and contributions to an interest bearing account that the inmate might use upon release from incarceration. However, in response to opponents who complained about competition with business, the legislation contained a number of restrictions: inmates must be paid the local prevailing wage and given comparable benefits; written assurances must document that non-inmate workers will not be displaced or severely impacted; and organized labor and local private industry must be consulted before startup. Given these restrictions, it is not surprising that private sector employment of prison labor has not grown significantly.

> *Because it leads to increased production of goods and services, prison labor helps spur the U.S. economy.*

Both supporters and opponents of prison labor agree the debate over prison labor is at a critical juncture; employment in prisons could increase greatly in the coming years as prison populations rise. Moreover, in recent years, there has been growing criticism of FPI, not only for competing with business, but also for how effectively they are carrying out their mission of employing prisoners. As a result, Congress has been looking carefully at the issue of prison labor, especially as it relates to FPI. Under the trade name UNICOR, FPI markets about 150 types of products and services to federal agencies, including furniture, textiles, electronic components, and engine repair. By mandate, FPI is limited to offering its goods and services to the federal government, with certain exceptions for approved state projects under the Prison Industries Enhancement (PIE) program. In return for this limitation, Congress has required that federal agencies purchase a portion of the products they need from FPI, even if the products cost more than they would from a private vendor. . . .

The benefits of prison labor

Prison labor has two main benefits. First, it reduces inmate recidivism, thereby reducing crime and lowering prison costs. Second, if done right, it produces "profits" which can be used to offset the taxpayer-financed costs of incarcerating prisoners.

> *Both supporters and opponents of prison labor agree the debate over prison labor is at a critical juncture.*

Studies have shown that inmates who work in prison industries or had vocational training have better outcomes when they are released from prison. Research suggests that the failure of ex-offenders to maintain employment may contribute to high recidivism rates. In 1991, the Federal Bureau of Prisons released an analysis of the Post Release Employment Project. More than 7,000 program participants were evaluated over a two-year period. The study found that those offenders who received training and work experience while in prison had fewer conduct problems and were less likely to be arrested the first year after release. In 1993, the New York State Department of Correctional Services conducted a study of release outcomes for offenders employed in the production of eyeglasses, which found that the vocational program was effective in lowering rates of probation failure and rearrest for program participants. At 12 months after release, 3 percent of program participants had been returned to department custody compared to 11 percent of the control group; and at 84 months after release, 34 percent of program participants had been returned to department custody compared to 54 percent of the control group. An

FPI study found that upon release from prison, workers were 24 percent more likely to obtain full-time or day-labor jobs during this time. Moreover, by the end of the first year of release, 10.1 percent of the comparison group inmates had been rearrested or had their conditional release revoked, compared with 6.6 percent of program participants. Further, 72 percent of program participants found and maintained employment during this period, compared with just 63 percent of comparison group inmates. The study concludes:

> It appears that prison employment in an industrial work setting and vocational or apprenticeship training can have both short and long term effects that reduce the likelihood of recidivism, particularly for men. . . . Therefore, correctional industries' work and training programs could help to reduce prison populations.

These studies are not surprising since statistics show that offenders are more likely to be unemployed at time of arrest. One study by the National Institute of Corrections found that up to 40 percent of all offenders were unemployed or marginally employed prior to arrest. A New York State Department of Labor study found that 83 percent of probation and parole violators were unemployed at the time of violation. Lower rates of recidivism are not just good for society by reducing crime, but also help keep prison populations smaller than they would otherwise be, saving taxpayers money.

These are criminals who are serving time in prison for illegal activity and, as such, are deprived of some of the rights free people enjoy.

Prison labor can also help offset the costs of housing prisoners, reducing taxpayer-financed costs while increasing GDP. When viewed from a growth economics perspective where the goal is to maximize national productivity and the output of goods and services, prison labor is a very good thing for the economy. The key to understanding this is to recognize that as new workers begin producing output, existing workers are not displaced permanently. They get jobs again and produce goods and services. In this case, the economy is better off because both civilian and prison workers are producing output. Supply creates its own demand. As these prison workers create output, a portion of the money returns to them and they consume items while in prison. But most of the money goes to reducing the costs of housing convicts, which in turn either allows taxes to be reduced or is used by the government to increase spending on other needed services. Either case raises demand for goods and services. In the case of tax cuts, consumers spend the money on goods and services. In the case of government expenditures, the government spends it on government services. Even if the companies pay less than minimum wage (which FPI opposes), the economy still benefits since the products sold will be cheaper, allowing consumers to spend their savings on other goods and services. In all these cases, when prisoners work, the economy is richer because more people are working. It is pretty simple. In the moderate term, employing prisoners doesn't raise unemployment but adds to the overall GDP.

> *The prison work environment is usually safer than the rest of the prison.*

Although some opponents might be willing to grant that in the moderate term employing prisoners is good for the economy, they might argue that the economy can't absorb new prisoners and that it will boost unemployment rates. Considering that seven million welfare recipients moved from welfare to work between 1996 and 2000 as the unemployment rate went down, it is clear that the economy can easily add several hundred thousand prisoners to the labor force over the next five years without increasing unemployment rates. In fact, as the experience of the late 1990s showed, increases in the labor force have no effect on the unemployment rate because new workers don't just work, they also become consumers.

What's the source of opposition to prison labor?

In spite of the significant advantages of prison labor to both society and inmates, there are two main factors motivating its opponents: concern that making prisoners work is exploitative and fear that it will displace civilian business and labor. Both concerns stimulated the initial restrictions on prison labor put in place at the beginning of the 20th century and are motivating legislative efforts in Congress and the states to restrict it today.

To this day, the image most people have of prison labor comes from movies like "Cool Hand Luke," where workers are exploited by a sadistic foreman as they cut brush by the side of the road or break big rocks into small rocks. As a result of the vestiges of these images, some people reflexively oppose prison labor because they fear a return of such exploitation. Liberals in particular are prone to see prison labor as benefitting some vast "prison industrial complex" while exploiting an oppressed proletariat who have been unfairly imprisoned. For example, one University of Massachusetts website devoted to prisoner rights wrote:

> Convicted kidnapper Dino Navarrete doesn't smile much as he surveys the sewing machines at Soledad prison's sprawling workshop. The short, stocky man with tattoos rippling his muscled forearms earns 45 cents an hour making blue work shirts in a medium security prison near Monterey, California. After deductions, he earns about $60 . . . for an entire month of nine hour days. "You know they're making money. Where's the money going to? It ain't going to us."

A recent article in the liberal journal, *American Prospect*, by University of Oregon professor Gordon Lafer decried the unfairness of prison labor, stating: "Prison workers can be hired, fired, or reassigned at will. Not only do they have no right to organize or strike; they also have no means of filing a grievance or voicing any kind of complaint whatsoever. They have no right to circulate an employee petition or newsletter, no right to call a meeting, and no access to the press." He complained that inmates are exploited because they get "no health insurance, no unemployment insurance, no vacation time." Lafer goes on to state that "prison labor is analogous to slave labor." He, like most liberal opponents, seems to miss the fundamental point: These are criminals who are serving time in prison for illegal activity and, as such, are deprived of some of the rights free people enjoy. Prisoners don't get vacations, that's why they are in prison.

Moreover, the reality is that prison labor looks like normal labor; workers sewing garments, building furniture, recycling computers, answering phones, etc. The prison work environment is usually safer than the rest of the prison. In many cases, workers volunteer for work, because it is a lot more interesting and financially rewarding than watching TV all day. And, at least in the case of private work in prisons, work sites are subject to OSHA inspections.

Notwithstanding this, many on the left feel that prisoners are often incarcerated unjustly (they either didn't really commit a crime, or they should not have been imprisoned for it) and as such, are victims of an oppressive state and profit-hungry corporations seeking to exploit their cheap labor. Many argue against prison labor on the grounds that we should do more to help the unemployed get jobs before they go to prison. Former Secretary of Labor Robert Reich states: "In other words, without really intending to do so, the nation is in the process of creating a giant jobs program for people who are likely to be unemployed. The only problem is, in order to be eligible for it, you've got to be in prison." Reich incorrectly assumes that prison labor is a substitute for civilian labor.

Finally, some on the left fear that if prison labor is expanded somehow there will be a greater incentive on the part of the state to put more people in prison through things like mandatory sentencing laws. In his campaign to end prison labor, Lafer concludes:

> Ultimately such stopgap measures [such as requiring prisoners to be paid prevailing wages] will be neither effective nor politically viable as long as correctional facilities continue to operate under the fiscal constraints imposed by mandatory sentencing laws. Building a consensus not only against the extensive employment of prisoners but also against mandatory sentencing laws will be a slow and arduous process, but we must undertake it if we hope to stop the expansion of prison labor before it gets much further. A "free market" economy ought to have no place for a vast army of prisoners undermining the wages of working people.

The reality is that there is no causal link between prison labor and higher incarceration. But Lafer and his fellow travelers essentially want fewer people put in prison so there will be less competition for civilian workers.

The second source of opposition stems from the fear that prison labor takes away jobs and business from civilian labor and businesses. Unions, businesses, and trade organizations have launched campaigns in the states and Congress to limit its expansion and even roll it back. They make the case that prison labor, especially as operated by FPI, is essentially unfair because it takes jobs from law abiding Americans and business from entrepreneurs. Opposition from businesses who lose contracts (and their conservative political supporters) is understandable. The fact that they are losing business to a government enterprise that employs prisoners at rock-bottom wages makes it doubly difficult for them to swallow. Likewise, workers who lose their jobs due to competition with prison labor feel particularly aggrieved.

> *The reality is that there is no causal link between prison labor and higher incarceration.*

Market displacement, however, doesn't mean that prison labor is not good for the nation nor that its benefits don't outweigh the costs. In fact, in many ways this debate is similar to the trade debate. While the evidence is clear that free trade helps grow the economy, it also hurts certain workers and firms in the short run. The same can be true with prison labor if the inmates are producing items that take work away from private companies (although prison labor has the advantage over trade in that it also results in more Americans working, whereas trade only changes the nature of the work, not the number of people working). The answer is to expand assistance for displaced workers and affected firms, not to stop prison labor.

One reason why opponents see prison labor as a zero-sum game that takes jobs from others is that their model of the economy is one in which there is a fixed amount of demand for goods and services. This fixed demand determines the number of jobs and amount of business. If another business fills the demand, the companies and workers originally fulfilling it will cut back on output and the economy will be no better off. Lafer states: "Prison labor must be opposed on the more durable basis that it threatens free labor."

According to Lafer, making prisoners work real jobs (making car parts, taking airline reservations, sewing shirts, etc.) as opposed to "carrying boulders from one side of the road to another . . . takes jobs away from people on the outside" and is "at its heart anti labor." Labor is not alone, as businesses wave the small-business flag to argue that prison labor takes from civilian business to support prison business. If there were a limited and immutable demand for auto parts, airline reservations, and shirts, then substituting prison labor for civilian labor would simply transfer jobs from one group of Americans to another with no net benefit. But, as discussed above, it is not as if resources laid off in the private sector remain dormant in perpetuity. The capital, labor, and entrepreneurial talents will be redeployed and produce wealth and income.

There is no doubt that in some cases prison labor, especially when conducted by prison enterprises like FPI, can result in companies losing contracts and some of their workers losing jobs. For example, in 1998, Glamour Glove, a Long Island, N.Y., maker of gloves, was in jeopardy of losing a portion of its government contracting when FPI decided to invest prison labor in glove manufacuring. Through legislative pressure, Glamour Glove was able to prevent this. In these cases, it is important to provide assistance to the workers and allow companies to make the adjustment, just as we do with companies negatively impacted by trade. But even if Glamour Glove or other companies were to lose their contracts, it is important to recognize that prison labor isn't simply a zero-sum game—it adds to overall economic output. As a result, when viewed from this growth economics perspective, it is clear that the opposition's prescription to keep these prison workers idle or, even worse, have them break rocks, does nothing to add to the economic output and wealth of our economy. When prisoners work, the economy is better off. The total economic output of society is larger than what it would be if those prisoners were just moving rocks.

The majority of Americans support prison labor because they believe that prisoners should help offset some of the costs of incarceration. It costs approximately $40 billion annually to incarcerate prisoners in local, state, and federal prisons. That works out to approximately $20,000 a year per prisoner. Surely prisoners can work and contribute something to help pay for this so taxpayers don't have to spend as much. Opponents of prison labor use the fact that some prison laborers are incarcerated for life with no chance of release to argue that the focus on reduced recidivism is a sham. The fact is that requiring a life-inmate to work and contribute a portion of his/her pay to room and board is consistent with the notion of the prisoner's responsibility to give something back to society as payment for his/her crimes.

What should be done?

In order to ensure that prison labor can expand, and to limit unfair competition with the private sector, Congress should take away the federal sourcing requirement of FPI, allowing federal inmates to produce and sell to both the private and public sectors. . . . There are two ways to do this.

First, FPI could simply be allowed to sell its goods in the private marketplace. However, there are several problems with this. In spite of the fact that FPI employs over 22,500 prisoners and had sales of more than $583 million in 2001, it made a profit of only $4 million and actually lost $12.8 million in 2000. This wouldn't be so bad if FPI was using some of its pre-profit income to pay for the upkeep of prisoners. Instead, while UNICOR itself is self-supporting, no "profits" from it were used to offset the costs of incarcerating the prisoners. In fact, by law, any profits must go back into the operation of UNICOR, not into offsetting federal costs of running prisons. FPI pays $26 million in staff salaries and an estimated $40 million to prisoners, but only $2.9 million toward restitution. In large part this appears to be the result of a conscious FPI strategy to focus specifically on low-wage jobs while keeping productivity low to employ more workers. According to Kathleen Hawk Sawyer, director of the Federal Bureau of Prisons,

> Low wages provide FPI the opportunity to operate in a labor intensive manner and to employ more inmates with less output of finished goods. The sales per inmate in FPI is one-third to one-fourth that of the private sector worker. . . . Our country imports tens of billions of dollars of products made in countries where the prevailing wage is either equal to, or lower than, what FPI pays its inmate workers.

Not surprisingly, total FPI wages (not just those the prisoners get to keep) range from 23 cents to $1.15 per hour. It is striking that even at these low wages FPI needs a mandatory sourcing requirement to sell to the federal marketplace.

There is another problem with FPI operations: It is employing workers largely in old economy sectors that will see employment declines in the next decade. Thirty percent are employed making clothing and textiles, while 26 percent make office furniture. According to the Bureau of Labor Statistics, employment in other sectors is expected to decline over the next 10 years due to trade and technology. The chances of released inmates getting work in these sectors is low. FPI has been slow to expand into new economy sectors that could include call center operations, electronics assembly, data entry, and others. Moreover, even in these sectors, workers are often contributing very little to the final value of the product. For example, much of their furniture is simply assembled by prisoners, who add very little value.

> *The majority of Americans support prison labor because they believe that prisoners should help offset some of the costs of incarceration.*

While there is a clear and compelling case to be made for more prison labor, to help both prisoners and society, it is not clear that FPI itself is working. In many ways this shouldn't come as a surprise. As a federal government agency, it doesn't have specialized knowledge in how to run a commercial business. Moreover, FPI has a built-in incentive to employ as many prisoners as possible, but not necessarily in occupations where inmates are likely to find jobs in the future or at wages that can offset the costs of the federal prison system. In addition, FPI has become so focused on expanding sales, even if the prisoners are doing little of the work and FPI is buying close to finished items, that they have moved away from their core mission: employing prisoners in jobs that give them skills and generate enough earnings to offset some of the costs of housing prisoners. But rather than seek to limit prison work as the protectionists want, a more effective alternative would be to let private companies hire federal prisoners. This is already the model in 36 states which let private companies employ state prisoners. However, there are several issues to be addressed before moving forward with this reform at the federal level.

The first is wage levels. Letting companies pay rock-bottom wages makes it difficult for prisoners to pay back some of their debt to society, either through victim restitution or offsetting the cost of their upkeep. Moreover, paying workers low wages provides little incentive for companies to organize production for increased output. On the other extreme, opponents want to require companies to pay the "prevailing wage," defined as the average wage civilian workers in these occupations are paid in their local area. But requiring companies to pay prevailing wages would make it difficult for companies to profitably employ prison labor. While it is true that the companies would save money by not paying benefits like unemployment insurance taxes and health care, it is also true that the costs of employing prisoners can be higher, given the greater difficulty in establishing an efficient plant set-up, higher risks, and greater transaction costs. Moreover, there is intangible risk that companies will be spurned by the public or boycotted by unions for hiring prison workers. As a result, the best solution, from both a sense of fairness and efficiency, is to require that prison employers pay at least the minimum wage. If prisons can negotiate a higher wage, they should have the ability to do so.

But rather than seek to limit prison work as the protectionists want, a more effective alternative would be to let private companies hire federal prisoners.

The second major issue concerns the extent to which FPI can compete with the private sector. The Sensenbrenner legislation (H.R. 1577) would require that, before introducing any new products, FPI would have to go through a daunting process of approval that only a former Soviet central planner could love. It would let FPI enter into the production of new products upon approval by their board. This approval must be based on a complicated study that takes into account factors such as the unemployment rate of the particular industry sector which produces what FPI wants to start producing (a figure that is by definition impossible to calculate), the projected change in federal demand for the product, and whether the product is trade sensitive. It precludes FPI from entering into new products if the product is "produced in the private sector by an industry which has reflected during the previous year an unemployment rate above the national average; or is an import-sensitive product," the latter of which is defined as a product where the import to domestic production ratio is greater than 25 percent. In a perverse way, the bill would limit production to those items that the nation is already strong in. In contrast, H.R. 1535, "The Prison Inmate Act of 2001," introduced by Reps. Frank Wolf (R-Va.) and Bobby Scott (D-Va.), takes the opposite approach. It would create an eight member "Foreign Labor Substitute Panel" that would allow FPI to enter into new products and services only if "the goods, wares, or merchandise proposed to be . . . produced . . . would otherwise be produced by foreign labor." In this case, workers would gain skills in industries that don't produce domestically, so when they get out of prison with these skills they would find it difficult, if not impossible, to find work in a U.S. company. Not only does this not help the inmates when they are released, it does little to help the economy by imparting skills that the economy needs.

At their core, both bills are based on the mistaken notion that prison labor hurts the U.S. economy and is unfair to civilian labor and businesses. And so, while Congress can't bring itself to completely eliminate the program because of its positive effects on inmates, they hope to erect enough draconian and bureaucratic barriers to limit the political fallout from having prison industries compete. And in order to keep prisoners doing something "productive," they want taxpayers to foot the bill. A better solution than erecting a host of bureaucratic hoops so that FPI avoids competing with any American business would be to let the market decide how to employ prison labor. Congress should allow private companies, under the supervision of FPI, to come into federal prisons and employ workers.

Finally, it is not clear that if Congress removed obstacles to companies employing prisons and if prisoners themselves had increased incentives to do so, there would be a significant increase in private sector employment. Given some of the barriers involved, it may be that many companies would choose not to employ prison labor. On the other hand, a recent study of prison labor employers found that companies generally view prison workers as productive and dependable. The bottom line is that, either way, we should remove barriers to companies employing prison labor. . . .

There is a lot that can and should be done to ensure that workers and businesses benefit in the New Economy. Opposing prison labor is not one of them. In fact, limiting prison labor would lower economic growth, while reducing the effectiveness of prisons to move prisoners to productive and law-abiding lives when they are released.

8

Prison Labor Harms Inmates and the Economy

Jane Slaughter

Jane Slaughter is a Detroit-based labor writer.

Prison labor programs exploit prisoners who have little choice but to work at low-paying prison jobs if they want to reduce their sentences. Moreover, claims that prison labor helps rehabilitate inmates are misguided. The work, which is usually menial, does not teach prisoners marketable skills they could use upon release nor does it instill a desire to work. Prison labor also hurts American workers, whose jobs are now going to inmates.

Start talking about "prison labor," and people tend to fall into two categories. One is appalled at the exploitation implied: workers locked up, overseen by guards, with no say in their wages, conditions, or anything else. But the other group sees a chance to "make prisons pay" and to get tough on crime. Back in the 1970s, Chief Justice Warren Burger called for turning prisons into "factories with fences." Today, Burger's words are coming true, with consequences that may be as serious for workers on the outside as for those who labor behind bars.

Inmate laborers

The number of prisoners who work for private, profit-making companies or state-controlled industries—around 80,000—is still

Jane Slaughter, "Captive Labor: Jobs Without Justice," *The Witness*, November 1998. Copyright © 1998 by *The Witness*. Reproduced by permission.

relatively small compared to the skyrocketing prison population.

But the numbers are growing fast, urged along by advocates in government and by companies who see prison labor as a closer-to-home alternative to production in Asia and Mexico.

"It's about time we stopped being ashamed of our resources and began putting them to work," says Representative Stephen Matthew, chair of a Congressional committee studying prison labor. Matthew says his goal is to have half of all prisoners holding down inside jobs by the year 2000.

Consider these trends:

- a phenomenal increase in the number of people behind bars—1.9 million today, driving towards one percent of the total population—propelled by the lock 'em up mentality prevalent in legislatures;
- fewer and fewer good jobs available, as the supposedly "booming" economy creates mostly low-wage or temporary or part-time jobs (or all three);
- welfare recipients forced into low-paid jobs in competition with other working-class people, under the heading of "welfare reform."

Then recall the rhetoric that conservatives use to describe members of what they call "the underclass"—"welfare queens" sucking up the tax dollars of hard-working citizens, criminals watching TV in jail, likewise on the tax dollars of those same law-abiding citizens. Given all this, it's not hard to believe that policy makers have in mind a two-pronged "solution" to the perceived problem of the underclass: low-paid, poverty-sustaining jobs for the women, even lower-paid jobs in jail for the men. As one advocate mused in an Internet posting, "[Prison] labor is the carpet under which can be swept those who fall out the bottom of the system, and it's a profit center as well! . . . It seems to be the only government-sponsored program that 'deals with' inner-city unemployment."

Slave labor

In a collection of essays by prisoners, *The Celling of America*, prisoner Paul Wright, co-editor of *Prison Legal News*, notes that Americans mistakenly believe that slavery was ended by the Thirteenth Amendment. In truth, Wright points out, "slavery and involuntary servitude" were abolished, in the words of the Constitution, "except as punishment for crimes whereof the party shall have been duly convicted." After the Civil War, it was common for newly freed slaves to be "duly convicted," sent to jail, and then leased out to private employers.

In the 1930s, spurred by Depression unemployment, Congress forbade the interstate transport of prison-made goods made for less than minimum wage, effectively shutting down the private use of prison labor. It was today's prison-building binge that once again sent lawmakers looking for ways to make money from convicts' work. In 1979, Congress created a program to help bring private companies into prisons. From 1980 to 1994, sales by prison industries, private and state-run, rose from $392 million to $1.31 billion, as the number of federal and state prisoners working in prison industries jumped by 358 percent. Some industry officials estimate that by 2000 prison industries' sales will hit $8.9 billion.

Some prisoner activists, such as Paul Wright, call prison work "slave labor," arguing that it is not truly voluntary. According to the American Federation of Labor and Congress of Industrial Organizations (AFL-CIO), 21 states have passed laws requiring prisoners to work, and federal prisoners are required to work as well. Just as important, taking a job can reduce your sentence, often on a day worked per day served basis, and not taking one can subject you to penalties that lengthen your sentence.

Even at the pitifully low wages paid, prisoners take jobs for the money. Alice Lynd, co-founder of a prisoners' advocacy group called Prison Forum in Youngstown, Ohio, explains, "I have a friend who gets $17 a month for tutoring. People working for Ohio Penal Industries get as much as $45 a month. It creates a class system within the prison as to who's got money for the commissary and who hasn't." One prisoner doing data entry at San Quentin said, "The food here sucks and a can of tuna fish costs 95 cents in the commissary, so I am really glad to have this job."

Pay

Courts have ruled that the Fair Labor Standards Act, which mandates the minimum wage for free labor, does not apply to government-employed prisoners. Federal UNICOR [an independent federal prison industries corporation] inmates are paid between 23 cents and $1.15 per hour, and up to 50 percent of that may be deducted. Private companies in prison are required to pay the minimum wage. Whatever the nominal wage, however, prisoners see only a small portion of it. Prison officials make deductions for room and board, taxes, family support, victim restitution, and savings for release. A Unibase employee at Lebanon Correctional Institution in Ohio, for example, makes 47 cents an hour for data entry, and a sewing machine operator at Soledad in California makes 45 cents.

If prisoners have incentives to take prison jobs, private companies have equally strong motivation to locate behind bars. A publication from the Department of Justice spells it out: "Inmates represent a readily available and dependable source of entry-level labor that is a cost-effective alternative to work forces found in Mexico, the Caribbean Basin, Southeast Asia, and the Pacific Rim countries."

> *It's not hard to believe that policy makers have in mind a . . . 'solution' to the perceived problem of the underclass: . . . [low-paid] jobs in jail for the men.*

Company executives delight that prisoner-workers never get stuck in traffic (though they are subject to periodic prison-wide lockdowns). Nor do they receive benefits or vacations. And they fit well with companies' focus on "flexibility"—available when needed for surges in demand, returned to their cells, with no unemployment pay, when the market sags. Prisoners can be fired for any or no reason, including back-talk, and they are not allowed to unionize, much less to strike.

On top of these incentives, the government often provides handsome subsidies to entrepreneurs, such as leasing them space at very low rates or subsidies to buy equipment. An ad from the Wisconsin Department of Corrections asks business owners, "Can't Find Workers? A Willing Workforce Waits."

Perhaps the most bizarre rationale for prison labor is that it keeps jobs in the U.S. "We can put a Made-in-the-U.S.A. label on our product," one executive told a Justice Department researcher. Companies argue that prison jobs would otherwise be done by workers in Sri Lanka or El Salvador. The president of multinational Unibase, with workers inside three Ohio prisons, says that keeping work in the state is part of his "sales pitch."

It's easy to imagine a scenario in which a worker loses his job, commits a crime out of desperation, and then ends up working for his former company in jail. But at least he's got the job, not the foreign competition!

Good for prisoners?

Occasionally an advocate of prison labor will claim it's good for prisoners (as opposed to state or private coffers). The idea is that prison jobs teach work habits to those who've seldom held a steady job. One study, for example, showed that inmates employed by Badger State Industries in Wisconsin had a 15 percent lower recidivism rate than other inmates.

But others doubt that prison work will help prisoners once they return to society. For one thing, prison employers tend to cherry-pick the "best" prisoners, those with work histories and good records. Many managers set up the hiring scene as much as possible like private-sector ventures, with applications and interviews. So those hired are those most likely to make it on the outside in any case.

Second, most prison jobs are specifically designed not to require marketable skills. The Justice Department passes along the advice of a manager at a South Carolina firm: "Keep it simple—put the least complex sewing jobs you have inside the prison." Alice Lynd points out, "Sewing blue jeans isn't done outside prisons, it's done overseas. When they get out they won't be able to run down to a plant and get a job."

> *Whatever the nominal wage . . . prisoners see only a small portion of it.*

Third, although punching a behind-bars time clock is said to teach a "work ethic," the stultifying nature of the low-skill job could also carry the lesson that work is something to be avoided at all costs.

With the American workforce already battered by downsizing, privatization, contracting out, and the dislocation of jobs to overseas factories, workers' organizations are becoming alarmed by the rapid growth of prison work. "Prison labor," says the AFL-CIO, "is being used today to perform work in both the private and public sectors ordinarily done by free workers."

Under the 1979 Prison Industries Enhancement law, private

companies who want to operate in jail must pay the "prevailing wage." They must consult with and win approval from union leaders in the area; their industry must be one with no local unemployment; and the local labor market should not be affected.

But as the examples below show, these rules are apparently ignored:

- In Arizona, a hog slaughtering plant closed down, costing union workers their jobs. The plant then reopened as a joint venture between the Department of Corrections and the state's Pork Producers Association.
- In Wisconsin, Fabry Glove & Mitten cut wages and slashed outside jobs by 40 percent after hiring inmates at the Green Bay Correctional Institution.
- In Utah, asbestos removal companies say that prison labor has virtually driven them out of business. "We find it ironic that they are putting an industry out of business that they are purportedly training people to work in," said a spokesperson.
- Companies in the government-supply business say that UNICOR's rapid expansion has cost 2,000 jobs in furniture-making since the late 1980s.
- A private prison run by Wackenhut in Lockhart, Texas, houses a company called LTI which assembles circuit boards for IBM and Texas Instruments. Wackenhut built LTI a brand-new facility (using prisoner labor) and charges the company a rent of $1 per year. To top it off, LTI gets a tax abatement from the city.

  But before this cozy arrangement, LTI operated a circuit board plant in nearby Austin, employing 150 workers. The company laid them all off and moved its equipment to Lockhart.
- DPAS, a literature assembly firm, closed its facility in Tecate, Mexico, in favor of San Quentin.

More prevention

Youngstown, Ohio, where Alice Lynd lives and works, was devastated by the steel mill closings of the 1980s. She helped found the Prison Forum group after Youngstown officials hailed the construction of a new "Supermax" prison there as a job-creation coup. Prison Forum has drawn up a platform on prison labor that would protect both imprisoned workers and those outside the walls. Besides banning the displacement of outside jobs, it would give prison workers the right to unionize and strike, or, at the very least, to report their grievances to an outside labor organization to advocate on their behalf.

Lynd is a Quaker whose long-time activism has ranged from union support to draft counseling during the Vietnam war. Her work with prisoners, she believes, is "consistent with traditional Quaker concerns; it has roots that go way back." Prison Forum includes a retired schoolteacher, professors of criminal justice and English literature, two steelworkers and the religious education director of a Unitarian church.

As an attorney, Lynd is able to work directly with prisoners while also taking education into the community. "People tend to think of criminals as people who are like barbarians," she says, "people who are outside the society. But most of them are going to return to society, and they may have a more difficult time than they had before to reestablish themselves in a constructive mode, rather than go from bad to worse." She wants to "assist by giving people hope, help them figure out how their future can amount to anything, how they will make it on the outside."

Unfortunately, she doesn't see prison jobs, in their current form, as a big part of the solution. "Some major plants will hire ex-convicts," she says, "but there are an awful lot of occupations where they're not going to.

"We need to do much more at the prevention end. Increasingly repressive prisons and longer terms are not meeting society's needs. Jobs, education, assistance to get off drugs are being shortchanged to try to deal with it at the wrong end of the problem."

9

Super Maximum Security Prisons Are Cruel and Inhumane

Vince Beiser

Vince Beiser is a writer for the Los Angeles Times. *He writes frequently on inmate issues and conditions in California prisons.*

Super maximum security prisons house the worst of the worst. But the stark isolation, lack of activities, and few opportunities for rehabilitation in these institutions are making these inmates even more violent and antisocial. Despite some reforms, many prisoners leave super max prisons poorly equipped to integrate into society. Until voters become concerned about the condition in which these inmates are living, we will be endangered by the release of angry, unbalanced prisoners back into society.

It's quiet in pod C5, deep inside Pelican Bay State Prison's Security Housing Unit, home to about 1,200 of California's most violent offenders. There are no sounds from outside, because there are no windows—only a skylight high overhead, through which gray daylight seeps into the bare quadrangle facing the pod's eight cells, stacked four on four. All that can be heard are a few subdued voices, and the occasional thunderous sound of a flushing toilet reverberating off the blank concrete walls.

This is not the crowded, clamorous kind of prison you see in the movies. The SHU, as it's known, is a starkly efficient place of electronically controlled doors and featureless concrete and steel. Occasionally, the monotony is punctured by bursts

Vince Beiser, "A Necessary Evil?" *Los Angeles Times*, October 19, 2003. Copyright © 2003 by the Los Angeles Times Syndicate. Reproduced by permission.

of noise and violence. Sometimes inmates scream at guards, other inmates, or themselves. Sometimes there is the clangorous racket of a recalcitrant prisoner being forcibly extracted from his cell. But most of the time, nothing happens. Almost nothing is permitted to happen. That's the idea of the SHU.

If you're an inmate in a regular prison—even a maximum-security prison, which the other two wings of Pelican Bay are—most days you can play basketball in the yard or cards in the day room, work in the laundry room or dining hall and take meals with the other men on your tier.

In the SHU, there are no jobs, no activities, hardly any educational programs and barely any human contact. You are locked in your 8-by-10-foot cell almost around the clock. You can't see the other prisoners in the cells adjoining yours, nor the guards watching from a central observation booth. Most of the time, all you can see through the fingertip-sized perforations in your cell's solid steel door is the wall of the eight-cell pod, the larger cage containing your cage. Guards deliver your meals. Once a day, the remote-controlled cell door grinds open, and you get 90 minutes to spend alone in a walled-in courtyard—a place more like the bottom of a mine shaft than an exercise yard. It's an environment about as restrictive and monotonous as human minds can design—and, perhaps, as human minds can tolerate.

> *It's an environment about as restrictive and monotonous as human minds can design—and, perhaps, as human minds can tolerate.*

Pelican Bay, which sprawls over 275 acres just south of the Oregon border, in a . . . region of misty mountains and ancient redwood forests, was among the first of a wave of new prisons equipped with ultra-restrictive "supermax" lockups that have proliferated nationwide in recent years. There are as many as 20,000 inmates housed in such facilities in at least 30 states.

California has three SHUs for men in its Pelican Bay, Corcoran and Tehachapi lockups, plus one for women in Valley State Prison in Chowchilla. They house about 3,000 convicts in all. But Pelican Bay is the one with the hardest cons and the harshest conditions, the end of the line for the inmates whom correctional officials call "the worst of the worst."

Like their counterparts in other states, California corrections officials say they need SHUs to control incorrigibly violent cons in the state's vast archipelago of prisons, teeming with nearly 160,000 inmates. While no one could argue with that goal, there are significant concerns about the tactic. For starters, it's not clear to what extent SHUs are indeed reducing prison violence.

Supermax prisons may breed danger

More disturbingly, there's a growing worry that supermaxes—long decried by prisoner advocates as dangerous to the mental health of inmates—may be breeding danger for the general public.

Psychiatrists, activists and some correctional officials say the intense isolation of supermaxes is producing prisoners who are uncontrollably furious and sometimes violently deranged. Most of those prisoners will one day be set free. In the past three years, in fact, nearly 1,000 California SHU inmates at the end of their sentences were moved to less-restrictive prisons for just a few weeks, and then released.

And at least 403 inmates were paroled without even that intermediate step: They were taken straight from the solitary cells where they spent years marinating in their rage, handed $200 in gate money and put on a bus to rejoin the rest of us.

"T.C.," a Pelican Bay SHU inmate who, like most of the nearly two dozen current and former SHU prisoners interviewed for this article did not want his name published, wrote: "How does society expect a person to act once he has been released from the SHU, in most cases after spending years back here? There are things that happen here which people out there are never aware of; these things tend to build anger and hate in some persons, and if these persons don't have anyone to talk to, or complain to, that anger and hate continues to grow. If that person paroles, he's now a human time bomb waiting to release all that anger and hate, waiting to explode."

You can hardly blame prison authorities for liking the idea of supermaxes. Prison guards are spit on, screamed at and assaulted daily. Reducing the chances of being stabbed in the neck with a sharpened toothbrush is understandably a higher priority for them than fretting over how solitary confinement might change an inmate's mood.

But America's supermaxes have been denounced as inhumane by organizations from the ACLU to the United Nations. Fistfuls of lawsuits have been filed in recent years challenging conditions in supermaxes from California to Massachusetts. Some have succeeded in forcing changes. . . . So far, the courts have upheld the constitutionality of supermax-style imprisonment. But just because they're legal doesn't necessarily mean they're good policy. In fact, Democratic state Sen. Gloria Romero of Los Angeles, head of the Senate's Select Committee on the California Correctional System, has launched a campaign to investigate how supermaxes are affecting prisoners—and the public.

> *If that person paroles, he's now a human time bomb waiting to release all that anger and hate, waiting to explode.*

No question the Pelican Bay SHU holds a great many extraordinarily malicious men. Most of California's top prison gang leaders are there, including such luminaries as Aryan Brotherhood shot-callers Paul "Cornfed" Schneider and Dale Bretches, the original owners of the dogs that mauled a San Francisco woman to death in 2001. The day before my visit there this year, a SHU inmate who was appearing in court stabbed his own lawyer with an ice pick–like shank he apparently had hidden in what a Pelican Bay spokesman referred to as his "keister."

How inmates wind up in the SHU

There is considerable debate, however, about whether everyone in the SHU deserves to be there. No one is in the SHU for crimes they committed on the streets; you get sent there for doing something while you're in prison.

This works in two ways. The first is straightforward: If you violate prison rules—say, being caught with drugs or for attacking another inmate—you can be sent to the SHU for a set period of time as punishment.

The second is more ambiguous: Simply being declared a member or associate of a prison gang lands you in the SHU—

indefinitely. About half the state's SHU inmates are in for this reason. Aside from getting paroled or going certifiably insane, the only way a "gang-validated" inmate can be released from the SHU is by "debriefing"—confessing everything he knows about other gang members, which entails obvious risks—or by convincing prison officials that he has been free from gang activity for six years.

"Prison gang members and associates are responsible for the largest percentage of violence in our institutions," says Steve Moore, the head of gang-related issues for the California Department of Corrections. "The idea is to extract those people from the general population."

Corrections officials and prisoners agree that California's half-dozen major prison gangs—Nazi Low Riders, Aryan Brotherhood, Black Guerrilla Family and several Latino factions—are behind a hefty chunk, though certainly not all, of the trouble in prisons statewide, from stabbings to drug dealing. And as the number of people cycling through the prison system has swelled in recent years, some of those gangs are believed to have begun forging increasingly close links with street gangs on the outside.

> *America's supermaxes have been denounced as inhumane by organizations from the ACLU to the United Nations.*

Activists and inmates, however, charge that the department's criteria for determining gang membership are overly broad, sending many undeserving inmates to supermax solitary. SHU inmates in Corcoran and Pelican Bay have staged two hunger strikes in the past two years over the issue, and Romero convened a hearing in September [2003] to investigate the corrections department's policy of identifying gang members. "I have very serious concerns about the validation process," Romero said at the hearing, held in Los Angeles. "In this time of constrained budgets, it's a good time to look at who is going into SHUs and whether they should really be there."

In response to these criticisms, Moore ordered a review of all gang validations. As of September, his office had looked at several hundred cases and found 17 that didn't pass muster.

Regardless of why prisoners are put in the SHU, perhaps the most pressing concern for the public is the inmates' mental states upon release. Dr. Stuart Grassian, a Boston psychiatrist who lectured at Harvard Medical School, has been studying the effects of solitary confinement for more than two decades, during which time he has examined more than 100 supermax prisoners, including 50 at Pelican Bay. His conclusion: Supermax prisons can literally drive inmates crazy.

"There are many scores of cases of people who never suffered psychiatric illnesses and developed them while incarcerated in supermaxes," he says. Other mental health professionals agree. "I've seen many prisoners with no history of mental illness who after some time in the SHU started cutting themselves," says Dr. Terry Kupers, an Oakland-based psychiatrist with decades of experience in prison work. "I've almost never seen self-mutilation among adult males anywhere else, but it's very common in SHUs." At the landmark *Madrid v. Gomez* federal trial in 1995 over conditions at Pelican Bay, even the prison's senior staff psychologist acknowledged seeing psychiatric deterioration among some SHU prisoners.

Supermax prisoners often develop similar symptoms, Grassian says. These include hallucinations; hypersensitivity to external stimuli; paranoia; panic attacks; hostile fantasies involving revenge, torture and mutilation; and violent or self-destructive outbursts, to the extent of gouging out one's eyes, smearing oneself with feces or biting chunks of flesh from one's own body.

> *There are many scores of cases of people who never suffered psychiatric illnesses and developed them while incarcerated in supermaxes.*

Take Matthew Lowe, convicted of armed robbery, assault on a peace officer and grand theft auto. During his three years in the Pelican Bay SHU, Lowe never got to the point of biting off pieces of his sizable biceps, but in other ways he fits Grassian's diagnosis of a mentally ill inmate. Lowe is a big guy in baggy jeans and a motorcycle-shop sweatshirt, with a tiny soul patch on his chin and tattoos on his neck and fingers. At 38, he has spent most of his life behind bars, but he says his time in the SHU changed him in a way prison never had before.

"Them years of sitting in that little cell—it did something to me, I don't even know what," says Lowe, sitting on a couch in his girlfriend's tidy bungalow in a blue-collar suburb of San Francisco. "I only had conversations with about five or six people in three years. I'd sit in there and just think about doing crazy [stuff] all the time. . . . Your average prison doesn't do that to you." After years of obsessively ruminating about blowing up buildings and shooting cops, Lowe was finally paroled last year [2002]. He was taken from his SHU cell, shifted to San Quentin for a few days and then let out onto the streets of Marin County.

So far, he's doing all right, working as a roof-gutter installer and going to AA meetings. But he scares himself with how jumpy and paranoid he has become. "So many times I've come so close to snapping since I got out," he says. "One time in a store, someone cut in front of me in line—a 50-year-old guy, I don't think he even realized it. I had to catch myself, because my first thought was just to smash him."

The roots of solitary confinement

Penal solitary confinement was essentially invented in the United States. In the late 1700s, whips and stocks were the preferred tools of public punishment. But reformers argued that by isolating criminals, their consciences would naturally lead to repenting their evil ways.

In 1790, Pennsylvania opened the first prison designed for this purpose, dubbed a "penitentiary." Several American states and European nations soon followed suit. But the penitentiaries gradually fell out of favor as evidence began to mount that they were often driving inmates mad. As the Supreme Court observed in an 1890 ruling condemning the penitentiary system: "A considerable number of prisoners fell, after even a short confinement, into a semi-fatuous condition . . . and others became violently insane; others still, committed suicide; while those who stood the ordeal better were not generally reformed."

Still, solitary confinement continued to be used as a short-term punishment for inmates. But the idea of keeping large numbers of convicts permanently in such severe conditions didn't return until the 1980s, as America's prison population began mushrooming. Driven largely by tough anti-drug and "three-strikes"-type mandatory minimum sentencing laws, the number of Americans behind bars has quadrupled since 1980 to an all-time high of about 2 million today. In the same get-tough-on-criminals spirit, many states have also cut back educational programs, exercise facilities and other "perks" for prisoners. Violence grew apace. Desperate to restore order to the federal maximum-security lockup at Marion, Ill., authorities in 1983 put the entire facility on indefinite lockdown. Under the administrations of then-Gov. George Deukmejian and then-Corrections Department head James Rowland, California was among the first states to copy the concept, opening SHUs at Corcoran in 1988, and Pelican Bay in 1989.

Mental health needs of inmates are ignored

Pelican Bay came under fire almost right away, both over alleged abuses by guards and conditions in the SHU. In the *Madrid v. Gomez* decision, U.S. District Court Judge Thelton Henderson ruled that there was a "pattern of brutality" by the guards. On whether the SHU itself was damaging to inmates' mental health, he ruled that while the SHU "may press the outer bounds of what most humans can psychologically tolerate" and could seriously exacerbate previously existing mental illnesses, there was not enough proof to show that it could drive a sane man mad.

Pelican Bay instituted several reforms as a result of the case, including creating a 127-bed psychiatric unit and beefing up its mental-health staff to a total of 79. As far as the prison was concerned, that took care of the problem. "We moved all of those with mental illnesses into the [psychiatric unit] after the Madrid decision," declares Rawland Swift, who, until recently, was the Pelican Bay spokesman. Certainly, the SHU's conditions aren't as extreme as those that so appalled the 1890 Supreme Court. Pelican Bay SHU inmates can talk to others in neighboring cells, receive letters and see visitors (through security glass) on weekends. Those who can afford them have TVs (though they can only watch during the day and must listen through earphones). Most occasionally leave their cells for brief excursions to court or for medical treatment.

A select number of SHU inmates even have cellmates, but most are housed alone, and the overwhelming bulk of their time is spent in a small concrete and steel box. It seems entirely possible that a good many SHU inmates are losing their grip on reality—whether their keepers acknowledge it or not.

Prisoners are given mental-health attention if their guards—hardly experts in such matters—deem their behavior strange enough to warrant an examination. Swift told me that while seemingly troubled prisoners are often taken to the psychiatric unit for evaluation, the psychiatrists almost always send them back, saying, "He's got a behavioral problem, not a mental health problem." This echoes disturbingly a finding of the judge in the *Madrid* decision: "It is clear . . . that an overburdened, and sometimes indifferent, mental health staff is far too quick to dismiss an inmate as a 'malingerer' and thus deny him needed treatment."

Almost all of the inmates I interviewed (and at least one correctional officer who did not want to be named) said they had seen other prisoners suffer serious mental deterioration in the SHU—screaming, banging on doors, cutting themselves. "I have seen plenty of people lose their sanity while in the SHU. I used to think that they were faking it . . . but once being around them for a while you could see that it was no act," writes Pelican Bay SHU inmate Otis Booker. "When you hear a guy holding a conversation with himself, or calling out cadences to exercises that he's not even doing or growling out animal sounds all day, you know something's not right."

> *Prisoners are given mental-health attention if their guards—hardly experts in such matters—deem their behavior strange enough to warrant an examination.*

Grassian estimates that as many as one-third of all supermax inmates are suffering some kind of psychiatric trouble—most of which goes undiagnosed. "A guard may see a prisoner hiding under a blanket, obviously delusional, but as long as he's not screaming or throwing feces, he's OK as far as they're concerned," Grassian says.

All of which could help explain the case of Erik Scott January, convicted of armed robbery. His mother, Long Beach resident Laura Daniher, says that before he was sent to the Corcoran SHU in 1997, January had no history of mental health problems. After a couple of years in the SHU, though, he started raving about the evil spirits he saw dancing on the walls.

In a letter to her from mid-2001, January writes relatively lucidly for most of two pages, asking about her house and other chitchat—and then mentions that he has been seeing things and experiencing other "strange occurrences." A few months later, another letter makes it apparent he has left reality far behind: "I am Tutankamen mother. . . . Take a time to pray to your hi Hitler power of white skin because I need some hand in time I need hand time handtime . . . god is the sun I am the sun I am Satan I am Lucifer."

Vanessa Filley, a member of California Prison Focus, a San Francisco–based advocacy group, visited January early last year [2002] and found him "in a delusional state," suffering "visual hallucinations." In a letter to the warden asking that January be taken out of the SHU, Filley states that she was told by a Corcoran psychiatrist that January "is not dysfunctional to the point of forced intervention, therefore barring any specific behavior we can't do anything." At the time of this writing, January was still in the SHU.

Certainly, SHUs don't drive everyone over the threshold of clinical insanity. But they may have dangerous effects short of that. What happens when you take a man who had antisocial and violent impulses to begin with, lock him in a cell by himself for five or 10 years, and then let him out?

"It's like keeping a dog that has bitten someone in a cage, kicking it and beating it all the time until it gets as crazy and vicious as it can be, and then one day you open the cage and run away," Grassian says. "Taking someone straight from the Pelican Bay SHU and sending them back to San Francisco or Los Angeles is about as dangerous a thing as you can do."

Even some corrections officials agree. "From my experience as a prison administrator, the prolonged confinement of inmates with little or no contact with others will only make people worse," Jerry Enomoto, a former California director of corrections, said when the *Madrid* lawsuit first hit the courts. (Current Department of Corrections director Ed Alameida did not respond to several requests for an interview.)

Some people, of course, are less affected by the SHU than others. But at best, it seems, coming out of the SHU often leaves prisoners dangerously ill-equipped to cope with the stress of being around other people.

"Tony" is a 30-year-old Latino and former gangbanger with a generous mustache and hair cropped so short you can see the scars on his head. He has done time in both the Corcoran and

Pelican Bay SHUs. Since his parole [in 2002], he has been living with his mom in a quiet Bay Area town and working as a diesel mechanic. On the spring afternoon I met him, an ancient little dog was asleep on a pillow in the front yard next to Tony's massive weight set.

Like Matthew Lowe, Tony was sent straight home from the SHU after a few days in San Quentin. "On my first day out, my mom took me to the grocery store," he says. "I blew up on a couple of people. There was some woman who came up about five feet behind me, and I turned and said, 'Don't stand so close to me!'" Months later, he still breaks out in hot sweats when he's out in crowds. The day before, he says he found himself moving warily away from an elderly woman standing behind him in line at the post office. "I'm not the same," he says. "Look at me, I'm paranoid of a 90-year-old lady in the post office. It's from being so isolated. No wonder people who've been in five or six years come out and kill people."

Released inmates pose a danger

There have been at least a few hair-raisingly brutal crimes committed by convicts fresh out of supermaxes. In 1992, one day after getting out of the Pelican Bay SHU, Robert Lee Davenport, 24, kidnapped, beat and raped a woman in El Cerrito. In 1995, within a week of his release from the same facility, Robert Walter Scully, 36, killed a Sonoma County sheriff's deputy, took hostages and barricaded himself inside a house in a standoff with police before finally surrendering.

Judging from the media coverage and conversations with people who remember these cases, it doesn't seem that anyone made the connection, or pointed to the SHUs as possibly having contributed to crimes committed by former SHU inmates. Grassian says he has served as consultant on more than a dozen similar cases nationwide. There may be more crimes to add to this list, but no one keeps track of what happens to SHU inmates as a group after they are freed to their parole officers. They are just another former con.

According to Department of Corrections statistics, killings in California prisons dropped dramatically in the years immediately after the Corcoran and Pelican Bay SHUs opened. But the total rate of assaults in the state prisons has been rising since. As of 2000, the inmate-on-inmate assault rate was just as high as in the years before the SHUs opened, and the rate of armed assaults on staff was even higher. Despite its oppressive security, there were 221 assaults in the Pelican Bay SHU [in 2002]—inmates assaulting guards when they are taken to court, for example, or by ingenious methods such as firing homemade blowguns through the perforations in their cell doors. More ominously, in the past [few] years federal prosecutors have charged more than a dozen members of two prison gangs with directing—via letters and visitors—scores of murders and attempted murders in prisons around the country from their cells in the Pelican Bay SHU.

Moore is aware of all this. But, he says, the SHUs are better than nothing. "We have much better investigative tools with the gang leaders in the SHUs," he says. "We know where they are. We can monitor them more closely. Will we ever totally stop them? No. But are we hindering them? Yes. And the best way we've found so far to do that is the SHU."

This is a common view among supermax supporters. Still, as a 1999 National Institute of Corrections report on these facilities points out, "There exists little or no hard data comparing such perceived impacts on entire systems versus the fiscal cost to gain such results." That's no small matter, considering how prodigiously expensive supermaxes are. Taxpayers forked over $218 million to build Pelican Bay, and spend $115 million every year to keep it running. It costs California about $28,000 per year to hold an average prisoner, but SHU inmates, with their elaborate security measures, cost substantially more. The Department of Corrections won't provide an exact figure, but most experts estimate the cost is as much as two or three times greater.

What can be done?

"We should definitely be looking at ways to reduce the number of inmates in SHUs," says state Sen. Romero, who visited Pelican Bay in June [2003]. "We may not like the fact that someone is a gang member, but is that a reason to throw them in this prison-in-a-prison? I'm not convinced of that, especially given the high costs." She aims to keep up pressure on the corrections department to modify its gang-validation policy, and to have more research done into what happens to SHU inmates after they are released.

It makes more sense, says Charles Carbone, an attorney with California Prison Focus, to deal with chronic violent offenders on a case-by-case basis, rather than shovel everyone who might be involved in violence into SHUs. "The purpose of the SHU can be served in each prison by administrative segregation," he says, referring to a type of solitary confinement that's not as restrictive and long. "But even then, those people should not be cut off from rehabilitative programs. In fact, they should get more. Cutting them off completely from all stimulation does nobody any good."

Psychiatrist Kupers, among others, believes the main cause of the surge in violence in the '80s was overcrowding and the idleness that resulted from programs being cut. "If you take everything away, prisoners become desperate, and therefore uncontrollable," he says. "Crowding, idleness and lack of rehabilitation cause violence. And no amount of supermaxes will stop that."

Even if you believe SHUs are necessary, Grassian says, they can be modified to make them more humane. In particular, Grassian recommends creating a transitional program to slowly reintroduce inmates to interaction with other people, something that happens in several other states. At present, with the exception of prisoners who are debriefed, the only pre-release preparation Pelican Bay SHU inmates are offered is a voluntary program that primarily consists of watching videos.

Making visits easier could also ease the transition, with prisoners housed in SHU facilities closer to home. Most experts agree that prisoners who maintain family ties generally do better after release. But Pelican Bay is a solid 14-hour drive from Los Angeles, its biggest single source of inmates; getting up there is a challenge for many families. "That visiting room is never full, even though there are over 1,000 people in the SHU," says Oakland resident Helen Grimes, who makes the trek almost every month to visit her son.

No such changes seem likely to happen soon, however. While the current state budget boosts corrections spending overall, it cut funds for inmate-related programs. Gov. Gray Davis understood well that most voters are not especially concerned about what happens to prisoners in SHUs or elsewhere. For them, the moral equation seems simple: Prisoners broke the law; let them suffer the consequences.

But most of the prisoners locked away in the maddening solitude of the SHUs will one day be freed to return to our midst—some of them angrier, more impulsive and more unbalanced than ever. And we will all have to live with those consequences.

Organizations to Contact

The editors have compiled the following list of organizations concerned with the issues debated in this book. The descriptions are derived from materials provided by the organizations. All have publications or information available for interested readers. The list was compiled on the date of publication of the present volume; names, addresses, phone and fax numbers, and e-mail addresses may change. Be aware that many organizations take several weeks or longer to respond to inquiries, so allow as much time as possible.

American Civil Liberties Union (ACLU)
125 Broad St., 18th Fl., New York, NY 10004
(212) 344-3005
Web site: www.aclu.org

In order to create constitutional conditions of confinement and strengthen prisoners' rights, the ACLU founded the National Prison Project in 1972. The organization remains the only national litigation program on behalf of prisoners. In its thirty-year history, the National Prison Project successfully represented over one hundred thousand confined men, women, and children. The project's class-action lawsuits improved care for prisoners suffering from tuberculosis, cancer, HIV/AIDS, and mental illness. The project has also changed prison policies that had led to gross overcrowding and protected prisoners from sexual assaults.

Amnesty International (AI)
322 Eighth Ave., New York, NY 10001
(212) 807-8400 • fax: (212) 463-9193
e-mail: admin-us@aiusa.org • Web site: www.amnestyusa.org

Amnesty International is a worldwide group of people who campaign for internationally recognized human rights. AI has a vision for a world in which every person enjoys all of the human rights enshrined in the Universal Declaration of Human Rights. In pursuit of its vision, AI's mission is to undertake research and action focused on preventing and ending grave abuses of the rights to physical and mental integrity, freedom of conscience and expression, and freedom from discrimination. The organization publishes numerous books and reports, as well as the monthly newsletter *Wire Newsletter*.

The Heritage Foundation
214 Massachusetts Ave. NE, Washington, DC 20002
(202) 546-4400 • fax: (202) 546-8328
e-mail: info@heritage.org • Web site: www.heritage.org

Founded in 1973, the Heritage Foundation is a research and educational institute whose mission is to formulate and promote conservative public policies based on the principles of free enterprise, limited government, individual freedom, traditional American values, and a strong national defense. The organization advocates tougher sentencing and the construction of more prisons. The foundation publishes articles on a variety of public policy issues in its *Backgrounder* series, *Heritage Lectures*, and its quarterly journal, *Policy Review*.

Human Rights Watch (HRW)
350 Fifth Ave., 34th Fl., New York, NY 10118
(212) 290-4700
e-mail: hrwnyc@hrw.org • Web site: www.hrw.org

Human Rights Watch is an independent, nongovernmental organization designed to investigate and expose human rights violations. HRW has conducted specialized prison research and campaigns for prisoners' rights since 1987 to focus international attention on prison conditions worldwide. They maintain that a government's claim to respect human rights should be assessed not only by the political freedoms it allows but also by how it treats its prisoners. The organization publishes several international publications, including its annual *World Report*.

National Center for Institutions and Alternatives (NCIA)
7222 Ambassador Rd., Baltimore, MD 21244
(410) 265-1490 • fax: (410) 597-9656
Web site: www.ncianet.org

The National Center on Institutions and Alternatives is a public benefit corporation founded in 1977. Since that time, the organization has been on the leading edge of new concepts in criminal and juvenile justice, providing professional research, training, and technical assistance for developing and supporting community-based programs. As a result, NCIA has developed and implemented sentencing programs in fifteen states, trained thousands of public defenders and their staffs, and prepared information for more than ten thousand individuals facing sentencing in adult and juvenile courts. Their organization staff members have written a number of publications, links to which are available on the NCIA Web site. They also publish a monthly magazine, *NCIA Research and Public Policy Report*.

National Crime Prevention Council (NCPC)
1000 Connecticut Ave. NW, 13th Fl., Washington, DC 20036
(202) 466-6272 • fax: (202) 296-1356
e-mail: webmaster@ncpc.org • Web site: www.ncpc.org

The National Crime Prevention Council's mission is to enable people to create safer and more caring communities by addressing the causes of crime and violence and reducing the opportunities for crime to occur. The organization provides training and education to help reduce crime. NCPC has many low-cost and free publications available, and publishes the monthly magazine *Catalyst*.

Prison Activist Resource Center (PARC)
PO Box 339, Berkeley, CA 94701
(510) 893-4648 • fax: (510) 893-4607
Web site: www.prisonactivist.org

The Prison Activist Resource Center is an organization committed to exposing and challenging the institutionalized racism of the criminal justice system. PARC provides support for educators, activists, prisoners, and prisoners' families. Their projects include building networks to expose human rights violations, and challenging the rapid expansion of prisons. PARC publishes a book, updated twice yearly, the *Resource Directory for Educators and Activists on the Crisis in Prisons.*

Prison Fellowship Ministries
1856 Old Reston Ave., Reston, VA 20190
(877) 478-0100 • fax: (703) 478-0452
e-mail: correspondence@pfm.org • Web site: www.pfm.org

Prison Fellowship Ministries is a nonprofit, volunteer-reliant ministry. The organization partners with churches across the country to minister to prisoners, ex-prisoners, and their families. Their focus includes fellowship with Jesus, teaching others to look at life from a biblical perspective, visiting inmates, and providing support to the children and families of prisoners.

The Sentencing Project
514 Tenth St. NW, Suite 1000, Washington, DC 20004
(202) 628-0871 • fax: (202) 628-1091
e-mail: staff@sentencingproject.org
Web site: www.sentencingproject.org

The Sentencing Project, incorporated in 1986, has become a national leader in the development of alternative sentencing programs and in research and advocacy on criminal justice policy. In the field of criminal justice policy, the organization is widely known for its reports and analyses highlighting inequities in the criminal justice system. The Sentencing Project has provided technical assistance and helped establish alternative sentencing programs in more than twenty-two states and consulted on issues such as juvenile detention, racial disparity, and the trial of juveniles in adult court. The organization has a number of publications on incarceration available on its Web site.

Bibliography

Books

Jeffrey Archer   *A Prison Diary*. New York: St. Martin's Press, 2003.

Jane Evelyn Atwood   *Too Much Time: Women in Prison*. London: Phaidon Press, 2000.

James H. Bruton   *The Big House: Life Inside a Supermax Security Prison*. Stillwater, MN: Voyageur Press, 2004.

David Cole   *No Equal Justice: Race and Class in the American Criminal Justice System*. New York: New Press, 2000.

Joel Dyer   *The Perpetual Prisoner Machine: How America Profits from Crime*. Boulder, CO: Westview Press, 2001.

Alan Elsner   *Gates of Injustice: The Crisis in America's Prisons*. Upper Saddle River, NJ: FT Prentice-Hall, 2004.

Jeff Evans, ed.   *Undoing Time: American Prisoners in Their Own Words*. Boston: Northeastern University Press, 2000.

David Garland   *The Culture of Control: Crime and Social Order in Contemporary Society*. Chicago: University of Chicago Press, 2002.

Robert Ellis Gordon   *The Funhouse Mirror: Reflections on Prison*. Pullman: Washington State University Press, 2000.

Marc Mauer and   *Invisible Punishment: The Collateral Consequences of Meda Chesney-Lind, Mass Imprisonment*. New York: New Press, 2003.
eds.

Donice Neal, ed.   *Supermax Prisons: Beyond the Rock*. Lanham, MD: American Correctional Association, 2003.

Christian Parenti   *Lockdown America: Police and Prisons in the Age of Crisis*. New York: Verso Books, 2000.

Joan Petersilia   *When Prisoners Come Home: Parole and Prisoner Reentry (Studies in Crime and Public Policy)*. New York: Oxford University Press, 2003.

Jeffrey Reiman   *The Rich Get Richer and the Poor Get Prison: Ideology, Class, and Criminal Justice*. Boston: Pearson, Allyn & Bacon, 2003.

Jeffrey Ian Ross and   *Behind Bars: Surviving Prison*. Indianapolis: Stephen C. Richards Alpha Books, 2002.

Lennie Spitale

Prison Ministry: Understanding Prison Culture Inside and Out. Nashville: Broadman and Holman, 2002.

Michael Tonry and Joan Petersilia, eds.

Prisons: Crime and Justice. Chicago: University of Chicago Press, 2000.

Stanley "Tookie" Williams and Barbara Cottman Becnel

Life in Prison. New York: SeaStar Books, 2001.

Jennifer Wynn

Inside Rikers: Stories from the World's Largest Penal Colony. New York: St. Martin's Press, 2001.

Periodicals

Kris Axtman

"Fight over Treatment for Sex Offenders," *Christian Science Monitor*, June 15, 2000.

Abby Ellin

"A Food Fight over Private Prisons," *New York Times*, April 8, 2001.

Herbert J. Hoelter

"When Hard Time Becomes Just a Waste," *Newsday*, August 25, 2002.

Reynolds Holding

"Sex in the Warden's Office," *San Francisco Chronicle*, February 16, 2003.

Barry Holman

"Masking the Divide: How Officially Reported Prison Statistics Distort the Racial and Ethnic Realities of Prison Growth," *NCIA Research and Public Policy Report*, May 2001.

Webb Hubbell

"The Mark of Cain," *San Francisco Chronicle*, June 10, 2001.

Wil S. Hylton

"Sick on the Inside. Correctional HMOs and the Coming Prison Plague," *Harper's*, August 2003.

Michael Isikoff

"Hard Time for Corporate Perps," *Newsweek*, December 20, 2002.

Ryan King and Marc Mauer

"Aging Behind Bars: 'Three Strikes' Seven Years Later," *Sentencing Project*, August 2001.

Christopher Lee

"Hiring Freeze Starts, Layoffs Possible at Bureau of Prisons," *Washington Post*, July 12, 2004.

Jerome G. Miller

"Juvenile Justice: Facts vs. Anger," *New York Times*, March 22, 2000.

Mary Mitchell

"Black Pols Get It Wrong in Backing Prisons over Schools," *Chicago Sun-Times*, June 10, 2004.

Claire Osborn

"Making Hard Time Easier: Off to Prison? Those Who've Been There Have Some Advice," *American Statesman*, January 13, 2003.

Tim Padgett

"When God Is the Warden: The Nation's First Faith-Based Prison Mixes Religion and Rehab—and Stirs Up Controversy," *Time*, June 7, 2004.

Jessica Reaves "The Land of Freedom Is Now Land of the Jailed," *Time*, April 20, 2000.

Peg Tyre "Nickel and Dimed: How States Keep Prison Costs Down," *Newsweek*, June 23, 2003.

John Wideman "Visiting Privileges: A Journey to the Son," *Washington Post Magazine*, July 11, 2004.

Ron Word "Inmates with HIV Face 'Downhill Slide,'" *Miami Herald*, July 11, 2004.

Index